LIVERPOOL EVERYMAN AND PLAYHOUSE
PRESENT THE WORLD PREMIERE OF

THE KINDNESS OF STRANGERS

BY TONY GREEN

LIVERPOOL EVERYMAN AND PLAYHOUSE

"Liverpool Playhouse and Everyman theatres are currently enjoying a fresh lease of life"

Independent on Sunday

Since January 2004, Liverpool Everyman and Playhouse have become full-time producing theatres once again, with a programme of homegrown work which alternates between the two venues, so that there is a continuous presence of theatre 'Made in Liverpool'.

Our aim is for these theatres to be firmly rooted in their community, yet both national and international in their cultural scope, offering audiences a rich and varied theatrical diet and putting Liverpool's theatre firmly back on the map. Recent, highly acclaimed productions have included Corin Redgrave in *The Entertainer*; Adrian Mitchell's adaptation of *The Mayor of Zalamea*; a co-production with Oxford Stage Company of Behan's *The Quare Fellow*; a rare double-bill of Noël Coward one-act plays, the European première of Dael Orlandersmith's Pulitzer-nominated play, *Yellowman* (which transferred to Hampstead Theatre); August Wilson's jazz-age drama *Ma Rainey's Black Bottom* and, in June, the world première of *Fly*, Katie Douglas's debut play.

Now, with *The Kindness of Strangers* and *Urban Legend* as the core of the Everyman's 40th birthday season, new plays and new writers are taking their rightful place at the heart of our programme. This theatre is at its best when it is a creative launchpad, and this intimate space provides a very special environment in which to experience a theatrical beginning.

This is an extremely dynamic period for the Everyman and Playhouse, with a major expansion in production, a passionate commitment to new writing, and a rapidly growing community programme. We believe that this expansion is the only appropriate response to the needs of the communities of Merseyside, to the great reservoir of local talent, and to the creative challenge of Liverpool's Capital of Culture status in 2008.

Gemma Bodinetz
Artistic Director

Deborah Aydon
Executive Director

For further information about our programme, please call 0151 709 4776, or see www.everymanplayhouse.com

LIFE BEGINS

Forty years ago a great theatrical tradition began in a crumbling ex-chapel on the corner of Hope Street. The Everyman was born on 28th September 1964, and quickly built a reputation for ground-breaking work. A succession of visionary directors, exciting writers, and bold acting companies kept the flame alive for decades, and the Everyman has been the crucible for an astonishing range of theatrical talent. This dynamic space has generated a prodigious range of shows, from new writing to reinvented classics, from music theatre to political drama, from the mad and the mischievous to the seriously seminal. Always ambitious, never predictable, the Everyman is a Liverpool original.

We feel the most fitting way to celebrate the Everyman's tradition of reinvention is by focussing on the future, with two world premières of new Liverpool plays, Tony Green's *The Kindness of Strangers* and Laurence Wilson's *Urban Legend.* These theatres are now passionately committed to supporting new writing, and we have a wide range of activities geared towards developing the plays and the playwrights of the future. If you would like more information on new writing at the Everyman and Playhouse – either as an aspiring playwright or as an audience member with a passion for the new – please contact our Literary Department on 0151 708 3700 or at literary@everymanplayhouse.com

Around these two premières we have sprinkled a range of other events which celebrate the Everyman's history, bring some great stalwarts back into the fold, and bring home some Liverpool plays that have enjoyed success elsewhere but not yet been seen in this city. And alongside the celebrations, we have set up the Life Begins Fund which will enable us to commission two new writers each year in the lead-up to Liverpool's Capital of Culture year 2008. The Life Begins lead funders are the Granada Foundation and the PH Holt Charitable Trust, and if you would like to support the Fund, please contact our Development Department on 0151 706 9115.

CRITICAL RESPONSE TO OUR RECENT PRODUCTIONS AT THE EVERYMAN

NICK BAGNALL AND JAMES WALLACE IN *THE MAYOR OF ZALAMEA*

The Mayor of Zalamea

"*A packed house and thunderous applause... This is a thrilling rebirth for an exciting theatre*"
THE SUNDAY TIMES

"*New artistic director Gemma Bodinetz begins her campaign at Liverpool theatres in vastly entertaining style*"
THE GUARDIAN

KEVIN HARVEY AND CECILIA NOBLE IN *YELLOWMAN*

Yellowman

"***** *Powerfully engaging*"
THE INDEPENDENT

"*Cecilia Noble and Kevin Harvey's dazzling performances are compassionate, intelligent and tough... Brighter than that Southern sunshine*"
THE TIMES

EVE DALLAS, DAVID JENKINS AND SIMON DONALDSON IN

Fly

"*If the quality of Fly is anything to go by, the Everyman's future looks bright.*"
DAILY POST

"*Katie Douglas's debut play… hooks the emotional heart of a situation and reels it in with dialogue as taut as a straining fishing line. *****"
THE GUARDIAN

Photography by Christian Smith

Also at the Playhouse...

The Entertainer

"***** *Very moving indeed*"
THE TIMES

The Astonished Heart and Still Life

"*Expertly acted (and) beautifully designed*"
THE DAILY TELEGRAPH

Ma Rainey's Black Bottom

"*Gemma Bodinetz's evocative, handsomely acted revival *****"
THE GUARDIAN

CREDITS

THE CAST (IN ALPHABETICAL ORDER)

Jimmy	Neal Barry
Stella	Diane Burke
Macy	Lorraine Burroughs
Behrouz	Sushil Chudasama
Mbusso	Alan Cooke
Sam	Tom Georgeson
Cheryl	Denise Gough
Shpetim	Talib Hamafaraj
Samir	Stefan Kalifa
Mohammed	Adam Levy
Cliff	Mark Rice-Oxley
Marvin	Mark Theodore

CREDITS

THE COMPANY

Writer	Tony Green
Director	Gemma Bodinetz
Designer	Soutra Gilmour
Musical Director	Tayo Akinbode
Lighting Designer	Natasha Chivers
Sound Designer	Sean Pritchard
Assistant Director	Nathan Miller
Dialect Coach	William Conacher
Costume Supervisor	Polly Lawrence
Casting Director	Julia Horan
Dramaturg	Suzanne Bell
Stage Manager	Robert Palfrey
Deputy Stage Manager	Sarah Lewis
Assistant Stage Manager	Rachel Garratt
Lighting Operator	Marc Williams / Mary Cummings
Sound Operator	Sean Pritchard
Set Construction	Liverpool Scenic Workshop Ltd.
Cover Image	Alexandra Wolkowicz

The Kindness of Strangers was commissioned by Liverpool Everyman and Playhouse and received its world première at Everyman Theatre, Liverpool, on 24 September 2004

With special thanks to: Fone Fix UK in Quiggins, 051, Masque, Catchy Monkey, Sunlight Services, Major Parr at Altcar Training Camp, Nail Nation

Approximate running time: *2 hrs 30 mins*

IN ASSOCIATION WITH

BBC RADIO MERSEYSIDE
95.8 FM – 1485 MW – DAB Digital Radio

CAST

NEAL BARRY
JIMMY

Neal trained at the Guildhall School of Music and Drama.

Neal's theatre credits include: *Sing Yer Heart Out for the Lads* (National Theatre); *A Christmas Carol* (Lyric Hammersmith); *Sweetheart* and *A Taste of Honey* (Salisbury Playhouse) and *The Way to Glory* (Chelmsford Civic Theatre).

Television includes: *The Bill, POW, Holby City, Serious and Organised, Silent Witness, Footballers' Wives, In Deep, 'Orrible, McCready and Daughter* and *Whistleblower.*

Television includes: *The Box*

DIANE BURKE
STELLA/SANDRA/
REGISTRAR

Diane's theatre credits include: *Snow White* (Camberley Theatre) and *Aladdin* (Crown Productions).

Television includes: *Brookside* (series regular).

Film includes: *Hell's Corner* and *Ice Cream Jesus.*

**LORRAINE
BURROUGHS**
MACEY

This is Lorraine's professional stage debut.

Lorraine's theatre credits whilst training include: *Caucasian Chalk Circle, The Crucible* and *Roberto Zucco* (RADA).

Film includes: *Red Rose* and *Hex*

Television includes: *Doctors, Down to Earth* and *Casualty.*

CAST

SUSHIL CHUDASAMA
BEHROUZ

Sushil's theatre credits include: *Kali Shorts* (Kali Theatre Company); *Krindlekrax* (Nottingham Playhouse and Birmingham Rep); *Mapping the Edge* (Wilson Wilson Company); *Queuing for Everest* (Sheffield Crucible); *As You Like It* (LAMDA) and *B22* (Royal Court).

Television includes: *Blue Murder, Casualty, Clocking Off III and IV, A & E, Doctors, Offside, Shipman, Strumpet, Cold Feet II, Cops II* and *Dream Team.*

Film includes: *Chicken Tikka Masala.*

Radio includes: *A Minus, Joe's Last Day, People Like Me, The Immaculate Conception, The Weaving Master, The Melamania* and *The Penalty.*

ALAN COOKE
MBUSSO

Alan's theatre credits include: *Ma Rainey's Black Bottom* (Liverpool Playhouse); *Medea* (West Yorkshire Playhouse); *Two Trains Running, The Day the Bronx Died, A Long Way From Home* and *All or Nothing at All* (Tricycle Theatre); *The Court Jester* and *Take Back What's Yours* (Croyden Warehouse); *A Night in Tunisia, One Step Beyond* (Stratford East); *Singer* and *Pericles* (RSC); *Glory* (Lyric and UK tour); *Sus* (Kings Head); *The Amen Corner* (Lyric); *Blood Brothers* (Bubble Theatre); *Jazz* and *The Blue Kitten* (Soho Poly Theatre); *The Wizard of Oz* (Birmingham Rep) and *Prez* (Hull Truck).

Television includes: *Doctors, Eastenders, In Deep, London Bridge, One Foot in the Grave, The Bill, Ronnie Corbett Show* and *Shakespeare Shorts – Macbeth.*

Film includes: *Young Adam, Shooting Fish, Death Wish III* and *I.D.*

TOM GEORGESON
SAM

Tom's theatre credits include: *The Seagull* (Edinburgh Festival); *Frozen* and *The Good Hope* (National Theatre and tour); *Lulu* (Almeida Theatre) and *Dealer's Choice* (National Theatre and Vaudeville Theatre).

Television includes: *Waking the Dead, Poirot: 'The Hollow', Foyle's War, Holby City, Ultimate Force, Clocking Off* (series IV), *Liverpool One* (two series), *Wuthering Heights, Between the Lines, GBH, The Manageress* and *Boys from the Blackstuff.*

Film includes: *Mandancin', The Virgin of Liverpool, Morality Play, Cause of Death, Land Girls, Swing, Downtime* and *A Fish Called Wanda.*

CAST

DENISE GOUGH
CHERYL

Denise trained at The Academy of Live and Recorded Arts (ALRA).

This is Denise's professional stage debut.

Denise's theatre credits include: *Robbers* (Actors Centre Tristan Bates Theatre), *Amadeus, Machinal, Angels in America* and *The Beau Defeated* (ALRA).

Television includes: *Lie with Me* and *Casualty.*

Denise won the Laurence Olivier Student Award in 2002.

TALIB HAMAFARAJ
SHPETIM

Talib was born in South-eastern Kurdistan (Northern Iraq). He graduated as a Primary Teacher in Suleimania in 1988 and taught for two years. For four years he was responsible for music and children's activities at the Mesopotamia Cultural Centre in Hewler, the Capital of South-eastern Kurdistan. As a singer, he has performed at festivals all over Kurdistan and has appeared on Kurdish television channels.

He left Kurdistan and arrived in the UK in 2000, seeking asylum. He has performed at Kurdish festivals all over the UK. As a singer and musician he has worked with the Greenhouse Project (Positive Images) which included workshops and cultural and musical demonstrations in primary and secondary schools around Liverpool.

Through singing he hopes to highlight the plight and demands of the Kurdish people, the largest stateless nation in the world.

STEFAN KALIPHA
SAMIR

Stefan's television credits include: *Dinotopia, Arabian Nights, Gulliver's Travels, The One that Got Away* and *The Hamburg Cell.*

Theatre credits include: *King Hedley II* and *Two Trains Running* (Tricycle Theatre); *Romeo and Juliet* (Birmingham Stage Company); *The Lion Fuente Ovejuna, The Coup* and *Measure For Measure* (National Theatre); *Hallelujah* (Riverside Theatre); *Don't Go Away Mad* (Donmar Warehouse); *Playboy Of the West Indies* (Court Theatre, Chicago).

Film includes: *The Jungle Book.*

CAST

ADAM LEVY
MOHAMMED

Adam trained at RADA.

Adam's theatre credits include: *Edmond* and *Henry V* (National Theatre); *Oh What A Lovely War, Romeo and Juliet* and *As You Like It* (Regents Park); *Crossing Jerusalem* (Tricycle Theatre); *Beauty and The Beast, Henry IV Part I, Back to Methusalah* and *Richard II* (RSC); *The Jew of Malta* (Almeida Theatre); *Salvation* (Gate Theatre) and *Conversations With My Father* (Old Vic).

Television includes: *10th Kingdom, McCallum, Call Red* and *Chillers – Prophesy.*

Film includes: *The Sin Eater, Gladiator, Being Considered* and *The Governess.*

MARK RICE-OXLEY
CLIFF

Mark trained at Webber Douglas.

Mark's theatre credits include: *The Entertainer* (Liverpool Playhouse); *Comedy of Errors* (Bristol Old Vic), *Cuckoos* (Barbican Pit and Ustinov Studio, Bath), *The Dwarfs* (Tricycle), *Workers Writes* (Royal Court), *The Danny Crowe Show* (Bush) and *Cressida* (Albery).

Television includes: *The Dwarfs, Merseybeat, Judge John Deed, In Deep* and *Two Pints of Lager and A Packet of Crisps.*

Film includes: George Harrison in *In His Life: The John Lennon Story, Lawrence of Arabia Close* and *The Streaker.*

Radio includes: *The Rake's Progress* and *Four For a Boy.*

MARK THEODORE
MARVIN

Mark trained at The Poor School.

Mark's theatre credits include: *Animal Farm, Edmund* and *The Collection* (Northern Stage); *Wrong Place* and *Dirty Butterfly* (Soho Theatre); *Measure for Measure* (National Theatre); *A Bitter Herb* (Bristol Old Vic); *Rumble Fish* (Pilot Theatre Company) and *Rise, All Over the Place* and *Nowhere Fast* (Tricycle).

Television includes: *The Bill, Casualty, Doctors* and *Queer As Folk II.*

Film includes: *Ali G in da House, NOD* and *Jamaica.*

COMPANY

TONY GREEN WRITER

Tony graduated from David Edgar's MA in Playwriting Studies at Birmingham University in 1998. He became an Associate Writer of the Liverpool Everyman and Playhouse in 2001, and was Writer on Attachment in 2002 when he first began work on *The Kindness of Strangers*.

His previous stage work includes *Permanent Damage* at the Unity Theatre, Liverpool – produced by Liverpool Lunchtime Theatre, directed by Paul Goetzee, 1996; (the same play received separate productions at The Questors Theatre and The Man in the Moon Theatre, London, in the same year). Also *Audrey,* a rehearsed public reading – directed by Max Stafford-Clark at Soho Theatre, London (2001).

Plays for radio include *It's A Wonderful Divorce* (Radio 4, 2001) and his short film, *Run Piglet Run!* (North West Vision and LA Productions) was recently shown at the Cannes Film Festival.

Tony received an Encouragement Bursary from the Arts Council of England in April 2002, and has attended workshops at the National Theatre and the RSC.

He is currently the fivearts Writer in Residence at the Liverpool Everyman and Playhouse and is working on his next stage commission, *Curfew*. He is also working on a screenplay of *The Kindness of Strangers* and is developing a TV series, *The Addict*, with Tailor Made Films.

GEMMA BODINETZ DIRECTOR

Gemma Bodinetz took up her post as Artistic Director for the Liverpool Everyman and Playhouse in September 2003. She has since directed *The Mayor of Zalamea* at the Everyman and *Ma Rainey's Black Bottom* at the Playhouse.

Gemma was previously an Associate Director at Hampstead Theatre. On completion of her study Gemma moved directly to The Royal Court Theatre. She left the Royal Court (London) to assist Harold Pinter on *The Caretaker,* returning to co-direct *Hush* with Max Stafford-Clark.

Gemma has directed numerous productions nationally. Her credits include: *Caravan* and *A Buyers Market* (The Bush Theatre); *Yard Gal* and *Breath Boom* (Royal Court, London); *Meat* (Plymouth Theatre Royal); *Hamlet* (Bristol Old Vic); *Luminosity* (RSC); *Rosencrantz and Guildenstern are Dead* and *Four Knights in Knaresborough* (West Yorkshire Playhouse); *Paper Husband, Chimps, English Journeys, Snake, Death Of Cool, Hand in Hand* and *After the Gods* (Hampstead Theatre); *Shopping and Fucking* (New York Theatre Workshop) and *Closer to Heaven* (West End). Her production of Jonathan Harvey's *Guiding Star* premièred at the Liverpool Everyman in 1998, before transferring to the National Theatre.

COMPANY

SOUTRA GILMOUR DESIGNER

Theatre credits include: *When The World Was Green* (Young Vic Theatre); *Animal* (Soho Theatre and tour); *Through the Leaves* (Southwark Playhouse and West End); *The Flu Season, Les Justes and Witness* (the Gate); *The Shadow of a Boy* (National Theatre); *Sun is Shining* (59e59, New York); *Hand in Hand* (Hampstead Theatre); *The Birthday Party* (The Crucible); *Fool For Love* (English Touring Theatre); *The Woman Who Swallowed a Pin* and *The Winter's Tale* (Southwark Playhouse); *Antigone* and *Therese Raquin* (Citizens Theatre); *Tear From a Glass Eye* (The Gate and National Theatre Studio); *Peter Pan* (Tramway, Glasgow); *The Mayor of Zalamea* (Liverpool Everyman); *Ghost City* (59e59, New York) and *Country Music* (Royal Court).

Opera and Ballet include: *The Girl of Sand* (Almeida Theatre); *Corridors* (ENO Bayliss Project); *A Better Place* (ENO Coliseum); *La Bohème* (Opera Ireland); *El Cimmarrón* (Queen Elizabeth Hall); *Bathtime* (ENO Studio) and *Eight Songs For A Mad King* (National and world tour).

Film includes: *The Follower* and *Amazing Grace*.

TAYO AKINBODE MUSICAL DIRECTOR

Tayo first discovered the theatre at the Activists Youth Theatre based at the Royal Court in London. After three years he moved to Manchester to become a stage technician and musician. In 1982 Manchester Youth Theatre asked him to compose music for their production of *A Midsummer Night's Dream*.

Theatre credits include: The BBC, Sheffield Crucible, Half Moon Theatre, Birmingham Rep, Red Ladder, Granada Television, and Bristol Old Vic and, most recently, *Mother Courage* at Nottingham Playhouse and on tour.

His recent work includes: *Yerma* and *Great Expectations* (Royal Exchange Manchester); *The Buddy Bolden Experience* (Royal Exchange Studio and Edinburgh Festival); *Beauty and the Beast* (New Vic); *Mother Goose* (Liverpool Everyman) and *Ma Rainey's Black Bottom* (Liverpool Playhouse).

COMPANY

NATASHA CHIVERS
LIGHTING DESIGNER
Theatre credits include: *Ma Rainey's Black Bottom* and *The Entertainer* (Liverpool Playhouse); *The Straits* (59e 59, New York, Paines Plough and Hampstead Theatre); *Very Little Women* (Lip Service tour); *On Blindness* (Paines Plough, Frantic Assembly and Graeae); *The Birthday Party* (Tag Theatre Company); *The Cherry Orchard* and *After The Dance* (Oxford Stage Company national tour); *The Bomb-itty of Errors* (The New Ambassadors); *Playhouse Creatures* (West Yorkshire Playhouse); *Peepshow* (Frantic Assembly, Plymouth Theatre Royal, Lyric Hammersmith and tour); *Wit* and *The Memory Of Water* (Stellar Quines, Tron, Traverse and tour); *Present Laughter* (Bath Theatre Royal Productions); *The Drowned World* (Paines Plough, Traverse Theatre and Bush Theatre); *Tiny Dynamite* (Frantic Assembly, Paines Plough, Lyric Hammersmith and tour); and *A Chaste Maid In Cheapside* (Almeida Theatre and tour).

SEAN PRITCHARD
SOUND DESIGNER
Sean is from Liverpool and studied Production and Performance Technology at The Liverpool Institute for Performing Arts before taking a job with the Everyman Theatre in 1999. He is currently Chief Technician at the Everyman.

Sound designs for the company include: *Fly, The Mayor of Zalamea, A Little Pinch of Chilli* and *'Master Harold'… and the Boys.*

NATHAN MILLER
ASSISTANT DIRECTOR
Nathan trained at Liverpool John Moores University and Hope Street Ltd. During this time, he directed Joe Orton's *What the Butler Saw* and *Bad Air Day*, which he co-wrote. Since leaving he has directed *Wonderland* (State of Flux), *Icarus* and *Closing Time* (Red Theatre) and *Battery* (Padded Cell). This is his first time working as Assistant Director.

COMPANY

WILLIAM CONACHER
DIALECT COACH

Recent theatre credits include:
Honeymoon Suite (Royal Court); *World Music* (Donmar Warehouse); *Six Degrees of Separation* and *Kes* (Royal Exchange); *One Flew Over the Cuckoo's Nest* (Edinburgh Festival and Gielgud); *The Postman Always Rings Twice* (West Yorkshire Playhouse); *Bat Boy: The Musical* (West Yorkshire Playhouse and Shaftesbury).

Other theatre credits include:
Crazyblackmuthafuckinself (Royal Court); *Singer, The Price* and *King Hedley II* (Tricycle); *She Stoops to Conquer* and *A Laughing Matter* (National Theatre); *The Woman Who Cooked Her Husband* (New Ambassadors) and *The Blue Room* (Haymarket).

William has also worked extensively in regional theatre, namely Theatr Clwyd, West Yorkshire Playhouse, Manchester Royal Exchange, the Library Theatre, Birmingham Rep, Sheffield Crucible and Chichester Festival Theatre.

Television credits include: *Faking It, Dead Gorgeous, Byron, Fallen, Hustle* and *Final Demand.*

Film credits include: *The Rocket Post, Topsy-Turvy, My Kingdom, Agent Cody Banks 2, Tristan and Isolde, White on White* and *Hooligans.*

William has been Dialect Coach at RADA since 1998.

POLLY LAURENCE
COSTUME SUPERVISOR

Costume designs for theatre include:
Scenes From an Execution (Embassy Theatre, London); *True or Falsetto* (Pleasance Theatre Edinburgh); *Searches* (BAC); *Patching Havoc* and *All Fall Away* (Latchmere Theatre) and *Hamlet* (Greenwich Theatre).

Designs for TV include: *How To Be A Man* and *Heavy.*

Assistant designs include: *Electra* and *Marieluise* (The Gate, London) and *Hamlet* (Edinburgh Festival).

SUPPORT US

The Liverpool Everyman and Playhouse are in the midst of a creative revolution: more new productions are now created here in Liverpool and there are more opportunities for talented writers and actors to be nurtured through our new writing and community initiatives. There is also a stronger presence of quality theatre on the city's cultural map and a higher profile on the national and international stage.

Our funding bodies and our audiences provide the grassroots support which ensures our survival, and we are sincerely grateful for it. But if we are to fulfil our ambitions for these theatres to flourish and blossom for future generations, we must be imaginative in raising support.

With your help, we can go further than these theatres have ever gone before.

By supporting the Everyman and Playhouse you will make it possible for us to create more spectacular work on both our stages; to nurture a new generation of actors and writers' to bring the best theatre makers to our city; to take Liverpool theatre far beyond home turf; and to reach out to our communities so that theatre can touch the lives of everyone on Merseyside.

For more details of how you as an individual, or your company, can be part of the growth and success of theatre in Liverpool, please see our website at www.everymanplayhouse.com, or contact our Development Department on 0151 706 9115 or at development@everymanplayhouse.com

Liverpool Everyman and Playhouse would like to thank all our current supporters:

FUNDERS

CORPORATE SPONSORS

Benson Signs; Bibby Factors Northwest Ltd; Brabners Chaffe Street; C3 Imaging; Chadwick Chartered Accountants; Dawsons Music Ltd; Duncan Sheard Glass; DWF Solicitors; Grant Thornton; Hope Street Hotel; HSBC Bank Plc; JST MacKintosh; Mando Group; Nonconform Design; Nviron Ltd; Oddbins; Synergy Colour Printing; The Famous Bankrupt Shop; The Workbank.

TRUSTS & GRANT-MAKING BODIES

The Eleanor Rathbone Charitable Trust; Liverpool Culture Company; P H Holt Charitable Trust; The Granada Foundation; BBC Northern Exposure; Channel 5 Televsion.

INDIVIDUAL SUPPORTERS

Peter and Geraldine Bounds, George C Carver, Councillor Eddie Clein, Mr & Mrs Dan Hugo, A. Thomas Jackson, Ms D. Leach, Frank D Paterson, Les Read, Sheen Streather, DB Williams and those who prefer to remain anonymous

 Liverpool Everyman and Playhouse is a registered charity no: 1081229

www.everymanplayhouse.com

STAFF

Ruth Adams Marketing Assistant, **Vicky Adlard** House Manager, **Duncan Allen** Finance Director, **Laura Arends** Marketing Officer, **Deborah Aydon** Executive Director, **Stephanie Barry** Deputy House Manager, **Rob Beamer** Chief Electrician (Playhouse), **Lindsey Bell** Technician, **Margaret Bell** Box Office Manager, **Suzanne Bell** Literary Manager, **Gemma Bodinetz** Artistic Director, **Pat Breen O'Neill*** Deputy Box Office Manager, **Tim Brunsden** General Manager, **Emma Callan*** Cleaning Staff, **Moira Callaghan** Theatre and Community Administrator, **Colin Carey*** Security Officer, **Stephen Carl-Lokko*** Security/Fire Officer, **Joe Cornmell** Finance Assistant, **Mary Cummings** Technician, **Emma Dyer** Box Office Assistant, **Roy Francis** Maintenance Technician, **Ros Gordon** Box Office Assistant, **Mike Gray** Deputy Technical Stage Manager, **Tony Green** Writer in Residence, **Helen Griffiths*** Deputy House Manager, **Fay Hamilton*** Box Office Assistant, **Jennifer Hawkswell*** Box Office Assistant, **Stuart Holden** IT and Communications Manager, **Lee Humphries** Press Officer, **Sarah Kelly*** Stage Door/Receptionist, **Steven Kennett*** Maintenance Technician (Performance), **Sven Key** Fire Officer, **Lynn-Marie Kilgallon*** Internal Courier, **Anthony Large*** Stage Door/Receptionist, **Robert Longthorne** Building Development Director, **Leonie Mallows** Box Office Supervisor, **Ged Manson** Cleaning Staff, **David McClure** Fire Officer, **Peter McKenna*** Cleaning Staff, **Jason McQuaide** Technical Stage Manager (Playhouse), **Louise Merrin** Marketing Manager, **Liz Nolan** Assistant to the Directors, **Lizzie Nunnery*** Literary Assistant, **Sarah Ogle** Marketing Director, **Sue Parry** Theatres Manager, **Joan Powell*** Cleaning Staff, **Sean Pritchard** Chief Technician (Everyman), **Keith Ranford*** Security/Fire Officer, **Collette Rawlinson*** Stage Door/Receptionist, **Rolande Roden** Development Manager, **Victoria Rope** Programme Co-ordinator, **Rebecca Ross** Theatre and Community Director, **Paula Rushworth*** Cleaning Staff, **Jeff Salmon** Technical Director, **Alistair Savage*** Development Assistant **Beverley Scott*** Box Office Assistant, **Rebecca Sharp** Annexe Receptionist, **Steve Sheridan*** Assistant Maintenance Technician, **Jackie Skinner** Theatre and Community Co-ordinator, **Nicky Sparrowhawk** Box Office Supervisor, **Jennifer Tallon Cahill** Deputy Chief Electrician, **Marie Thompson*** Cleaning Supervisor, **Hellen Turton*** Security Officer, **Paul Turton** Finance Manager, **Joan Uttley*** Press and Media Officer (Temporary Cover), **Deborah Williams** House Manager, **Marc Williams** Deputy Chief Technician, **Emma Wright** Technical Manager.

*Part-time staff

Thanks to all our Front of House team

Associate Writers:
Maurice Bessman, Helen Blakeman, Stephen Butchard, Katie Douglas, Shaun Duggan, Dameon Garnett, Tony Green, Judith Johnson, Jonathan Larkin, Nick Leather, Jan McVerry, Chloë Moss, Lizzie Nunnery, Mark Roberts, Esther Wilson, Laurence Wilson

Board Members:
Professor Michael Brown (Chair), Mike Carran, Vince Killen, Anne Morris, Roger Phillips, Sara Williams

Company Registration No. 3802476 Registered Charity No. 1081229

Thanks to our Interact team:
Christian Adeniran, Mickey Chandler, Vinnie Cleghorne, Peter Coker, Ms Dianne Crawford, Judith Cummings, Paula Frew, Patrick Graham, Caroline Hanson, Jane Hill, Justine Jenkins-Burke, Ms Kim Johnson, Mr M Kelly, Donna Ojapah, Chief Martin Okuboh, Edward Terry, Eugene Weaver and Robert Weaver

Interact is a voluntary group of people working to improve cultural diversity in our theatres as both audience members and employees. If you are interested in becoming a member of the Interact team or need more information please call the Marketing department on: 0151 706 9106 or write to

THE KINDNESS OF STRANGERS

First published in 2004 by Oberon Books Ltd
521 Caledonian Road, London N7 9RH
Tel: 020 7607 3637 / Fax: 020 7607 3629
e-mail: oberon.books@btinternet.com
www.oberonbooks.com

ISBN: 1 84002 496 8

Cover by Nonconform Design
Photograph by Alexandra Wolkowicz

Printed in Great Britain by Antony Rowe Ltd, Chippenham.

So I have a new name – refugee.
Strange that a name should take from me
My past, my personality and hope.
Strange refuge this.
So many seem to share this name, refugee,
Yet we share so many differences.
I find no comfort in my new name.
I long to share my past, restore my pride,
To show I too, in time, will offer more
Than I have borrowed.
For now the comfort that I seek
Resides in the old yet new name
I would choose.
Friend.

Ruvimbo Bungwe, 14
(*Amnesty International* magazine, July/August 2003.)

'People migrate today for the same reasons that tens of millions of Europeans once left your shores – they flee war or oppression, or they leave in search of a better life in a new land... The vast majority of immigrants are industrious, courageous, and determined. They don't want a free ride. They want a fair opportunity. They are not criminals or terrorists. They are law-abiding. They don't want to live apart. They want to integrate, while retaining their identity.'

Kofi Annan
(Speech to the European Parliament, January 2004)

'The poor man's Paradise – is a little peace.'

Blanche DuBois
Tennessee Williams, *A Streetcar Named Desire*

Characters

MOHAMMED Reza Ahmadi: 30, Iraqi Kurdish Refugee, from Halabja.

MACEY Lewis: 25, mixed race, prostitute.

CLIFF Dooley: 30, waiter and student.

CHERYL Tiernan: 22, student, musician, agoraphobic, thin.

JIMMY Baker: 38, bistro owner.

THE TROUBADOURS:

SAMIR Ashadi: 50, Iranian Refugee (accordion player), walks with a limp.

BEHROUZ Meszaros: 22, Iranian Refugee (guitar player).

SHPETIM Robaj: 24, Albanian (guitar player).

MBUSSO Thomas Sibanda: 40, Zimbabwean Refugee (double bass player), huge bear of a man.

SAM McDonald: 50, landlord.

MARVIN Cook: 24, black, fit, well-built, good-looking, Sam's 'muscle'.

STELLA McCann: 18, market trader, attractive.

POLICE CONSTABLE: (non-speaking).

IMMIGRATION OFFICER: (non-speaking).

REGISTRAR: 30s, female.

SANDRA: 30s – neighbour of Macey's.

'HOODED YOUTHS' can be played by cast members or stagehands.

Setting

Apart from one short scene at Dover, the play is set entirely in Liverpool.

Time

The present. Autumn.

Staging

There are 30 interior and exterior scenes, so the play would benefit from a pared-down style of presentation, with non-naturalistic staging. Scene changes should be done quickly, employing cast as well as stage hands. The music should be performed live.

For Annie

*(and for those people who were generous enough
to share some of their experiences with me:
Bala, Abrar, Adnan, Izzeldien, Amango, Abdellatif, Fadil,
Fadoul, Blend Jalal, Ismail, Kareem, Majid, Behrang,
Behrouz*, Mbusso* and Shpetim*)*

** These people are not the characters in the play
– I just 'borrowed' their names.*

PRE-SHOW

THE TROUBADOURS are performing outside the theatre. They are a group of musicians – refugees/asylum seekers: two acoustic guitars, double bass, accordion. MOHAMMED is with them, collecting money. If passers-by are charitable, then each night's takings will be donated to the following charities: ASYLUM LINK, REFUGEE ACTION, SUPPORT for ASYLUM SEEKERS and THE NATIONAL COALITION of ANTI-DEPORTATION CAMPAIGNS.

ACT ONE

Scene One

Darkness. Strains of a violin filter through: a rich, haunting melody. High up, at the back of the stage, a woman appears in silhouette, through her bed sit window. This is CHERYL. She is the violinist.

Lights up slowly on CLIFF and MOHAMMED either side of the stage. CLIFF is at his dresser. He is wearing a silk robe. He's in the process of applying make-up. A bottle and glass of wine on the dresser. MOHAMMED, wearing crumpled and tattered old clothes, all his worldly belongings in a hemp sack by his side, is on his knees, head bowed, praying.

CLIFF: It has often been remarked that the poor man's Paradise is a little peace. (*Pause.*) Have you any idea how humiliating it is for a single girl, a girl quite alone in this world, to suddenly find herself without a place to call her own? Is that completely beyond your comprehension?… A single girl and homeless… Homeless.

The sound of a tenbur (Kurdish stringed instrument) accompanies the violin… along with the sound of seagulls.

MOHAMMED: You see cliff which are white, you know is England. Is thing we know. White cliff mean safety.

Suddenly a brick is thrown onto the stage.

FIRST YOB: (*Off, Scouse accent.*) Fuck off Paki!

MOHAMMED starts, gets to his feet. Pause.

MOHAMMED: At Dover man say Mohammed is go to Liverpool. I ask what is like, Liverpool? Man say, you feel right at home. I say, is like Kurdistan? Man say, worse. I no understand. Man say, I give advice. Advice for Mohammed is, 'Do not drink water. Water come from dirty river. Water in Liverpool make people crazy. At night, when moon is big in sky, people in Liverpool, they have sex with goat…and relative who is nearest.'… Man say,

'You feel right at home.'… Mohammed is here six month, I no see one goat.

Another brick is thrown onto the stage. MOHAMMED jumps again.

SECOND YOB: (*Off.*) We said – Fuck off Paki!

MOHAMMED picks up both bricks.

MOHAMMED: Mohammed build new life in England. In Liverpool.

Scene Two

JIMMY's flat. Night.

JIMMY at his kitchen table, chopping vegetables. He reacts suddenly to a shooting pain in his temples.

JIMMY: Christ!

MACEY enters in bra and pants, drying her wet hair. She is holding her skirt and top, which she puts on during the scene.

MACEY: Why didn't yer warn me about the shower? Bloody thing's got a mind of its own. Hot cold hot cold scalding freezing. I haven't danced so much since I was a…stripper. … What's the matter with you?… You all right?

JIMMY: Bastard migraine.

MACEY: I'm not surprised. Think yer were over-doing it a bit. Man your age.

JIMMY: I'm thirty-eight.

MACEY: Exactly. Yer wanna be more careful. Looked like yer were trying to catch the last bus home.

She takes a swig from his bottle of lager. He throws her a look.

MACEY: D'yer always take so long to come?

She takes a piece of vegetable from the bowl.

JIMMY: Hey, help yourself why don't you.

MACEY: Thanks. (*She sniffs.*) Here…can I smell…is that *quiche*? Are yer cooking?

(*Looks at her watch.*) It's three in the morning. (*Pause.*) What yer chopping vegetables for this time of night?

She goes to take another piece of vegetable, JIMMY moves the bowl out of her reach. Pause.

MACEY: They said yer were a bit moody.

JIMMY: Who said I was a bit moody?

MACEY: The girls. We do talk to each other you know. We talk all the time.

JIMMY: Office gossip.

MACEY: Something like that.

JIMMY: Who's got the biggest cock.

MACEY: It ain't you. Mean and moody. Don't talk much. Very quiet when he comes.

JIMMY: And a small cock.

MACEY: … Not that small.

JIMMY: It's all right, you don't have to massage my ego. I'm a big boy.

MACEY: Not that big.

Beat. He smiles. Pause.

MACEY: Yer married?

JIMMY ignores her.

MACEY: Been in prison?

JIMMY ignores her.

MACEY: Long way from home aren't yer? Believe it or not, I've never had a cockney before. Had a Welshman once. That was weird… So. What brought yer to Liverpool?

JIMMY: I came up here for the scintillating conversation.

MACEY: All right, sarky arse.

JIMMY winces and puts a hand to his temple.

MACEY: Have yer taken anything for that? Got some
Nurofen in me bag.

She roots in her bag, gives him a Nurofen tablet.

JIMMY: Well, one's not going to do much good is it?

MACEY: It's me last one. Which bloody charm school did *you*
go to?

JIMMY washes the pill down with lager.

D'yer get them a lot?

JIMMY: Unfortunately.

MACEY: Might be a tumour.

JIMMY: Thanks.

MACEY: Happened to an uncle of mine. Six months of
headaches, thought it was stress, turned out to be this
big…cauliflower on his brain. Served him right, pervy
bastard.

JIMMY: Well it was nice making your acquaintance. Don't let
me keep you.

He pushes some money towards her.

MACEY: Right. Yer know where to get me if yer want me.

*One of MACEY's three mobile phones begins to ring. She looks
at the caller, answers it.*

Whoever it is, what yer doing out of bed? Daryl… What's
the matter? No…no, it's just a dream sweetheart, that's all.
A bad dream. There's no one… Listen to mummy now…
Daryl… There's no one hiding in the wardrobe, sweetheart.
You imagined it. That's all. (Bloody videos.) Where yer
sisters? Well you get back into bed too. Go on. Mummy
will be home soon. Few more hours in the factory then
I'll…yeah… Well, it's a chocolate factory, course I'm
gonna bring yer chocolate home… And I'll make yer a

nice brekky then take yer to school… OK… yeah… Mummy loves you too.

MACEY turns off her mobile, prepares to leave.

JIMMY: Hey Marcey…

MACEY: Macey.

JIMMY: Macey. You interested in making a little extra money?

MACEY: … Doing what?

JIMMY: Sit down.

MACEY: (*Picks up a courgette.*) I'm not into any mad weird stuff.

JIMMY: It's not weird stuff.

MACEY: I don't do videos.

JIMMY: It's not videos.

MACEY: And I don't mess with drugs.

JIMMY: Neither do I. Sit down.

MACEY hesitates, then sits, pops a piece of veg into her mouth.

JIMMY: How would you like to make an easy thousand?

MACEY: … Go on.

Blackout. Sound of fireworks – bangers mostly. A 'brick wall' descends. A hooded youth appears. He takes a can of spray paint from inside his top and, in large white letters, sprays the following onto the wall: PACKIES GO HOME!

Scene Three

Tower block flat. Night.

SAMIR is picking out the tune of The Beatles' 'All You Need Is Love' on his accordion. SHPETIM is going through the chord shapes on his guitar. BEHROUZ eats from a bag of very hot chips, acoustic guitar at his feet. (Occasional and distant sound of fireworks throughout this scene.)

BEHROUZ: Is like Arabic I think... (*Blows on his chips, eats.*) ...you think is like Arabic? Samir?

SAMIR: What is like Arabic?

BEHROUZ: Language here. Is like Arabic.

SAMIR: Is English.

BEHROUZ: I know is English. But *sound* like Arabic. (*Exaggerated Scouse:*) 'Chick-k-k-en.' 'Wick-k-ked.' 'Know what I mean, lik-k-ke.' Is all at back of throat. Is very strange.

SAMIR: Pick up guitar, Behrouz. Practise song.

BEHROUZ: I know song. Is easy. Boy in chip shop, he say, 'What the fuck-k-k you look-k-kin' at yer fuck-k-kin' Pak-k-ki?!'

SAMIR stops playing and looks at him.

BEHROUZ: No. Is OK. Was little boy.

SAMIR: You need be careful, Behrouz.

BEHROUZ: Little boy with big mouth. I say to him, 'I am from Iran.' You know what he say? 'You're still a fuck-k-kin' Pak-k-ki!' Is crazy.

SAMIR: You should no go chip shop at night.

BEHROUZ: I had big hungry.

SAMIR: You want brick throw at you?

BEHROUZ: No worry.

SAMIR: You want firework throw at you?

BEHROUZ: Behrouz too quick. Behrouz is like shit off shovel.

SAMIR: ... *What?*

BEHROUZ: Is expression. You want chip?

SAMIR: No.

BEHROUZ: Shpetim?

SHPETIM takes a handful of chips.

SAMIR: And you should no be eat their food, Behrouz.

BEHROUZ: Why?

SAMIR: Food is bad.

BEHROUZ: No Samir. Food is good. I like. 'Jock-k-kies.' (*He laughs.*) I hear old man call them 'jock-k-kies'. Is crazy language. You think is crazy language Shpetim?

SHPETIM shrugs his shoulders.

BEHROUZ: I bet you could not translate into Albania.

SAMIR: There is no health in this food.

BEHROUZ: But it have good taste.

SAMIR: You should look after body.

BEHROUZ: What you talk? I have fantastic body.

SAMIR: In six month these are word you no use.

BEHROUZ: You want feel? My body is wick-k-ked. You want feel my body?

SAMIR: In six month you have great big belly.

BEHROUZ: Behrouz fit as fuck-k-k. I hear this today. Girl on street, she run, man say she fit as fuck-k-k. Behrouz fit as fuck-k-k also. I show you. Sit up. Push up. Walk on hand. I do everything. You watch.

BEHROUZ starts doing push ups. MOHAMMED enters, out of breath, holding a bottle of water and some papers.

MOHAMMED: I look…for Dr…Andrei.

BEHROUZ: I do this with man on back.

MOHAMMED: You see…him?

SAMIR: You have strong arm, Behrouz. But your belly, it will touch ground.

MOHAMMED: You see…Dr Andrei?

BEHROUZ: Mohammed, you sit on back. I give you ride.

SAMIR: Lift is broke again, Mohammed?

MOHAMMED nods 'Yes'.

BEHROUZ: I no need lift. I run up stair. Three at one time.

MOHAMMED: Samir, I must…speak with Dr Andrei… You know where I find him? Is big important.

BEHROUZ: Behrouz fit as goat on mountain.

SAMIR: Be quiet, Behrouz. I think Andrei is make translation somewhere.

MOHAMMED: *I* need him make translation!

BEHROUZ: All I need is girl now, I have big fun!

SAMIR: … What is problem, Mohammed?

MOHAMMED: I get letter. From Home Office. Look.

BEHROUZ: You know, is prostitute by garage who take voucher. I hear this. She take voucher, show you good time.

SAMIR: You stay away from prostitute, Behrouz.

BEHROUZ: (Stay away from food…stay away from prostitute.)

MOHAMMED: Is all in English. What it mean Samir?

BEHROUZ: I live life of old man!

SAMIR: Behrouz, Shpetim, go find Mbusso. We rehearse new song.

BEHROUZ: We rehearse *now*? Is time for *Emmerdale*.

SAMIR: You watch too much TV Behrouz. Is bad for brain. Go find Mbusso.

BEHROUZ groans and exits with SHPETIM.

MOHAMMED: What this letter mean, Samir? (*Gives him the letter…*) Many many many word. But is not in my language! So how I know what mean?

SAMIR: Is difficult. Is language of lawyer.

MOHAMMED: Is not good. I have feeling. In stomach. Is not good news.

SAMIR: You must show solicitor.

MOHAMMED: Solicitor is no good. He no read document, he no understand, he just get money. Is all he care. We stay he get money. We go home he get money. Dr Andrei will help. He is good man.

SAMIR: Yes. Andrei is good man. But he is *doctor*. Not lawyer. For this you need solicitor.

MOHAMMED: Dr Andrei tell me he know many big people. Important people. He have contact. He know how to make thing right.

SAMIR: Mohammed. My friend. Listen to me. You have plenty trust. Too much trust I think. You need be careful. OK?… Be careful friend… Find new solicitor.

MOHAMMED: Where to find? Tell me that, Samir.

BEHROUZ bursts in…

BEHROUZ: Samir! Come! Come with quick!

SAMIR: What is, Behrouz?

BEHROUZ: Mbusso! He up on roof. He drunk, Samir. Very drunk. He pissed as fart… Is expression. Come!

The three of them exit.

Scene Four

Split scene: Tower Block Roof / Street below.

Darkness. MBUSSO singing. An African song: 'Rain, rain, beautiful rain' by Ladysmith Black Mambazo. He has a rich, deep, impressive bass voice.

Fireworks illuminate the night sky, revealing MBUSSO standing on the ledge of the tower block roof. He is drunk, holding a half bottle of whisky. SHPETIM is on the roof watching MBUSSO.

'Down below', a fire is burning in an old oil drum. It illuminates two hooded youths: one of them is spraying racist graffiti on a wall: ASSYLIM SKUM FUCK OFF HOME. The other youth is hanging a crude effigy of an asylum seeker from a lamp post.

SAMIR, BEHROUZ and MOHAMMED arrive to join SHPETIM on the roof.

SAMIR: Mbusso… ? Come down from there my friend. Mbusso ..?

BEHROUZ: Mbusso! Are you fucking crazy!

SAMIR: Sshhh Behrouz!

MBUSSO continues to sing.

MOHAMMED: Why he sing for rain? I no understand.

BEHROUZ: Because he is one crazy fucker. *That* is why he sing for rain. OW! Why for you hit?

SAMIR: Keep mouth close, Behrouz! Mbusso… Mbusso… please be careful friend.

MBUSSO stops singing, turns to look behind him, teeters dangerously.

SAMIR: Come down now, Mbusso. Please. We have new song to learn. We have –

MBUSSO silences him with a raised hand. A moment. MBUSSO looks skyward…rain begins to fall on him. 'Down below' the hooded youths have finished their business and departed. Lights slowly down, the last image visible being the hanging effigy. Sound of bangers, off.

Scene Five

CHERYL's bed sit.

Darkness. Sound of dripping water into a bucket. The sound of pizzicato violin in counterpoint to the dripping water. Lights up on CHERYL, alone in her bed sit. She's plucking notes on her violin as she watches the water drip into the bucket. She does this for a while and then grows bored. She looks over at her dresser, where a large but inexpensive BIRTHDAY CARD is on display. She puts down her violin and picks up the card. She opens it. She returns the card to the cabinet then picks up an old T shirt and begins tearing it into strips. She's interrupted by a knock at the door...

CLIFF: (*Off.*) Cheryl? (*Pause.*) Cheryl, it's Cliff. (*Pause.*) Cheryl, are you in there?

CHERYL: Where else would I be?

CLIFF: (*Off.*) Can I come in?

CHERYL: What d'yer want?

CLIFF: (*Off.*) I've brought you a cup-a-soup.

CHERYL: I never asked yer for a cup-a-soup.

CLIFF: (*Off.*) I was having one and I just thought... I've got some magazines for you... Can I come in?

CHERYL: If yer must.

CLIFF enters, carrying a mug, and a plastic bag.

CLIFF: Cream of vegetable. Your favourite. (*Takes magazines from the bag.*) Cosmo. My favourite.

He tentatively takes out two library books, puts them on the bed. Pause.

CHERYL: What's with the books?

CLIFF: I've been to the library.

CHERYL: Have yer now?

CLIFF: I just thought...

CHERYL: What?

CLIFF: ...You know.

CHERYL: I know what?

CLIFF: Research.

CHERYL looks at the books...

CLIFF: I thought maybe we could read them together…talk it through…and, you know, maybe we can come up with some kind of plan. (*Pause.*) They're very good. They were recommended by Raj Persaud.

CHERYL: Friend of yours, is he?

He holds up a Cosmo. *Little pause. Suddenly, CHERYL tears a page from one of the books… and begins making a paper aeroplane.*

CLIFF: Cheryl! What the…that's a bloody library book!… What are you doing?!

She sends the paper plane flying into the air.

CHERYL: Research?… That's what I think of yer research.

Pause. CLIFF retrieves the paper plane, unfolds it, and returns it to the book.

CHERYL: Yer can go and *shite* with yer research.

CLIFF: You know, it's all very well telling me to go and shite…but *what* are we going to do?

CHERYL: We?

CLIFF: You then.

CHERYL: It's none of yer feckin business what *I'm* going to do!

CLIFF: … I'm only trying to help.

CHERYL: I never asked for yer help. And I don't *need* yer help.

CLIFF: You've got no money left, Cheryl.

CHERYL: Didn't I tell yer not to come meddling into me life?

CLIFF: You can't do this on your own.

CHERYL: Do *what* on my own?… I'm happy on my own. Can yer not get that through yer head?

Pause.

CLIFF: So, you don't need me for anything? You don't need anyone? Rent. Food. Life's little luxuries. (*Picking up a piece of torn T shirt.*) Not to mention the essentials. I'm not blind you know. And I'm not stupid. Here… (*Takes a box of tampons from the plastic bag…*) I hope I got the right size. (*Pause. From the bag:*) Evening Primrose Oil. My mother used to swear by it… Chocolate. Every woman I know swears by it. (*Pause.*) D'you need any pain killers?

… She nods… He goes to leave.

CHERYL: Cliff……… thanks.

CLIFF: You're welcome.

CLIFF leaves. Blackout.

Scene Six

Jimmy's Bistro.

Bohemian style. MOHAMMED and SAMIR sit at a table. SAMIR is smoking, MOHAMMED is drinking from a bottle of mineral water. Off to one side – a mop stands in a bucket. They sit in silence. CLIFF enters with a cup of coffee. He's wearing a T shirt with the logo: 'BE YOURSELF, ONLY BETTER'.

CLIFF: One coffee. Extra strong.

SAMIR: Thank you.

CLIFF: You could stand your tea spoon up in that.

SAMIR: Please?

CLIFF: Never mind.

SAMIR: You would like me to pay now?

CLIFF: It's OK. It's on the house.

SAMIR: House?

CLIFF: Free.

SAMIR: Why you give for free?

CLIFF: No reason.

SAMIR: I have money. I pay for coffee. I no want for free.

CLIFF: O… K. (*To MOHAMMED.*) Are you sure I can't get you anything?

MOHAMMED: I am happy with water. Thank you. Is soon for Mister Jimmy you think?

CLIFF: It's difficult to say. He tends to come and go as he pleases. Anyone would think he owned the place.

MOHAMMED: I have interview with Mister Jimmy.

CLIFF: (*Confused.*) Interview?

SAMIR: Appointment.

CLIFF: I don't think there are any vacancies at the moment.

MOHAMMED: Please?

CLIFF: There's a few cafs on Bold Street. You might want to try there.

MOHAMMED: (*To SAMIR.*) I no understand.

SAMIR: (*To CLIFF.*) We just wait for Mister Jimmy. Thank you.

CLIFF: Ah. Well. Your wait is at an end. Here comes Sleeping Beauty now.

JIMMY enters carrying a box of provisions.

CLIFF: Afternoon.

JIMMY: Don't start.

CLIFF: You'd think with all this beauty sleep you'd look like Johnny Depp or something. Instead of –

JIMMY: Cliff, I mean it, don't start with me today. I'm really not in the mood. I've got the migraine from hell.

CLIFF: Yes. And I've got a class at eleven.

JIMMY: What class?

CLIFF: I told you. I told you last week. The tutor couldn't – I'm not telling you all this again. I'm out of here at a quarter past and I won't be back till after two.

JIMMY: I've got no one else on this morning. Diane's not coming in till three.

CLIFF: Not my problem.

MOHAMMED comes over…

JIMMY: When are you going to pass this bloody course anyway? You've been doing it since you were twelve or something.

CLIFF: Fuck you.

MOHAMMED: Hello…you are Mister Jimmy? (*Holds out his hand.*) I am Mohammed.

JIMMY: (*Ignoring his hand.*) Wait at your table. I'll be with you in a minute.

MOHAMMED: Andrei Strahkov, he make telephone, yes? He say I should see you. Mister Jimmy. 10 o'clock. At bistro. Is more than 10 o'clock.

JIMMY: Wait at your table.

MOHAMMED discreetly shows JIMMY a bulging brown envelope under his jacket.

MOHAMMED: I bring what you say. What Andrei say. Is all here.

JIMMY: Mohammed, do you understand English?

MOHAMMED: I have little.

JIMMY: Then go and wait at your table.

MOHAMMED returns to his table.

CLIFF: Just a daily ray of sunshine aren't you?

JIMMY thrusts the box at CLIFF.

JIMMY: Here. Put these in the back. And leave the quiche alone.

CLIFF thrusts the box back at him.

CLIFF: You put them in the back! I've got my mopping to finish. And incidentally, why is 'Meester Jeemy' suddenly so popular with asylum seekers?

JIMMY: Mind your own business.

JIMMY exits with the box. CLIFF resumes his mopping.

MOHAMMED: Mister Jimmy has bad mood. You think I make him bad mood?

SAMIR: Try and be relax Mohammed.

JIMMY enters, jacket off, sits at table with MOHAMMED and SAMIR.

MOHAMMED: I sorry, Mister Jimmy. Big sorry. I do something wrong.

JIMMY: Forget it.

MOHAMMED: No. You make talk with man and I…

JIMMY: It's OK.

MOHAMMED: Please forgive. Mohammed excited. When you walk in bistro. (*Little pause.*) This friend Samir. I am thanks, Mister Jimmy, what you do for me. I am big thanks. I give you money now?

MOHAMMED takes the bulging packet from his coat, puts it on the table.

MOHAMMED: Is all there. I sell everything come here. Home. Small land. Necklace and bracelet which belong mother.

JIMMY: I don't want to know.

MOHAMMED: Necklace was present from father.

JIMMY: Mohammed, I don't want your sob story. All right?

MOHAMMED: What is sob story?

SAMIR: Mister Jimmy just wants to do business.

MOHAMMED: Is all there Mister Jimmy. You count.

JIMMY: I don't need to count it.

MOHAMMED: Five thousand.

CLIFF is edging closer to the table, trying to eavesdrop...

MOHAMMED: You find me girl everything be OK, yes?

JIMMY: Not necessarily.

MOHAMMED: I live here then, no more problem.

JIMMY: It's not a guarantee Mohammed.

MOHAMMED: Doctor Andrei say you find me nice girl. He say you are man –

JIMMY holds his hand up to cut him off, turns to CLIFF.

JIMMY: Cliff, why don't you go polish the cutlery or something?

... CLIFF exits.

MOHAMMED: You find me nice girl then everything hunky dokey.

JIMMY: Mohammed, listen to me.

MOHAMMED: I like girl with dark hair. And big eyes. Nice big eyes.

JIMMY: I've found you a girl who will do this, but it doesn't mean that everything is –

MOHAMMED: You find girl already? So soon?

JIMMY: I have someone in mind.

MOHAMMED says something in Kurdish, a short grateful prayer. He rises and kisses JIMMY on both cheeks.

MOHAMMED: She is nice girl, yes? Big eyes? Is pretty?

JIMMY: Yes she's pretty.

MOHAMMED: You have picture?

JIMMY: No I don't have a picture.

MOHAMMED: Is small? Better she small.

JIMMY: She's a woman, that's all that matters.

MOHAMMED: I like small woman.

JIMMY: Mohammed, I'm not running a dating agency here.

MOHAMMED: Please?

JIMMY: Look. Her name is Macey. And she'll agree to marry you. But just –

MOHAMMED: Macey. Is nice name. Macey.

JIMMY: She will marry you. But just to help you try and stay in the country. You understand?

MOHAMMED: Stay in country yes. I want stay in country. Britain is great. England great. Liverpool very great.

JIMMY looks to SAMIR…

SAMIR: Mohammed, this girl, Macey, she is girl for business.

JIMMY: … Did Andrei explain all this to you?

MOHAMMED: I understand. Sure. Is girl for business. Is girl to help Mohammed stay in country.

JIMMY: That's right. But even this is no guarantee.

MOHAMMED: You come my flat soon. I cook big food for you. You like kebab Mister Jimmy?

SAMIR: How many people you help like this?

JIMMY: So far…four.

SAMIR: Mohammed is five?

JIMMY: Yes.

SAMIR: And how many stay in country?

JIMMY: Two.

SAMIR: Two.

JIMMY: Which is why it's important Mohammed understands. Getting married is only the half of it. We have to convince the home office that the two of them have a history. Otherwise –

MOHAMMED: Home Office! I hate Home Office. Home Office say Mohammed tell lie. But I no tell lie. You believe, Mister Jimmy? Mohammed no have lie in heart. Mohammed no have lie in tongue.

JIMMY: (*To SAMIR.*) The appeals stage, from what I can gather, it's something of a lottery. It all depends on who hears his case.

SAMIR: Is a lot to pay for lottery ticket.

Pause.

MOHAMMED: I see this girl soon, Mister Jimmy? This Macey. I like see my wife.

JIMMY: Sunday afternoon. 2 o'clock. You come here. I'll introduce you to Macey. I'll cook you a meal.

MOHAMMED: Yes Mister Jimmy. Yes. Sunday. 2 o'clock Mister Jimmy. I no be late.

MOHAMMED rises and exits. SAMIR hangs back.

SAMIR: Mohammed put trust in you. *You* understand?

JIMMY: He'll get what he's paid for.

MOHAMMED and SAMIR exit. JIMMY takes the money from the envelope and looks at it. CLIFF enters, jacket on, bag over his shoulder, and eating a wedge of quiche.

CLIFF: Right. I'm off.

JIMMY: (*Heading for the kitchen.*) That's coming out of your wages.

CLIFF gives him the finger.

JIMMY: You know what you can do with that.

CLIFF gives him two fingers.

JIMMY: And that one.

CLIFF mouths 'Oh fuck off!' and exits.

The 'brick wall' descends. The hooded youth appears, can in hand. This time he sprays: KEEP ENGLAND WITE!

Scene Seven

MACEY's Flat. Kitchen. Afternoon.

Darkness. Sound of a doorbell being pressed repeatedly … then heavy knocking. Lights up on MACEY and MARVIN. On the table, a saucepan with some baked beans and a wooden spoon in it; a pot of tea and a mug, a milk bottle, a ceramic jar with a lid, a rag doll. On the floor, a box containing toys and children's books. MACEY is in her dressing gown, looks sleepy. MARVIN is counting some cash.

MARVIN: Is this it?

MACEY: It's all I've got.

MARVIN: But it's not enough.

MACEY: I've got bills to pay.

MARVIN: Who hasn't? Come on, don't mess me about, I need the rest of it.

MACEY: I'm telling yer, that's it. That's every last penny.

MARVIN: You're having a laugh.

MACEY: Yeah, me sides are splitting. Yer not the only one in the queue.

MARVIN: You what?

MACEY: Look –

MARVIN: No. *You* look. I've bought you as much time as I can, but I'm telling you, he doesn't give a shit about your bills. And he doesn't give a shit about your kids not getting the latest pair of Nikes. He just wants his bread. He's funny that way. He likes his rent paid on time. And you're behind. Way behind. And that makes him very… irritable. And when he gets like that the grief gets passed on to me. And I've got enough on my plate.

MACEY: My kids have had nothing but baked beans the last three weeks.

MARVIN: (*Looking around.*) I'm supposed to break something.

MACEY: I'll have the money tomorrow. I will. I Promise. All of it. I'll clear the whole debt. I've got something lined up.

MARVIN: Lottery ticket?

MACEY: Something definite. Honest. He was supposed to be here, but, I don't know, something must have happened. (*Little pause.*) Tomorrow, yeah?

MARVIN: Tomorrow's too late, love. You're supposed to stick to the arrangement.

MACEY: I'm trying.

MARVIN: Not hard enough.

MACEY: How can I stick to the arrangement when he keeps putting the frigging rent up?

Pause.

MARVIN: Look at you, it's three in the afternoon and you're still in your dressing gown. Get a job for God's sake.

MACEY: Four pound an hour. How's that going to help me? (*Pause.*) I don't suppose…?

Pause. It dawns on MARVIN what 'suppose' means…

MARVIN: Have some self respect.

MACEY: I can't afford it. (*Pause.*) Just give me twenty four hours. One lousy day for chrissake. (*Pause.*) Oh, go on then! Break something. Break whatever yer want… Go on! Break the telly. Break the coffee table. Just stay out of the kids' rooms.

Pause. MARVIN takes the wooden spoon from the saucepan, licks it clean, then breaks it.

MARVIN: I'm warning you, he'll turf you out on the street. And your kids. And he won't bat an eyelid. In fact, he'll probably smile while he's doing it… Tomorrow.

MACEY: Tomorrow.

MARVIN exits. Pause. MACEY opens the ceramic jar and takes out a solitary five pound note – all she has in the world right now… She goes to eat some beans from the saucepan…but can't face them. Little pause. She picks up the rag doll. Pause. Sound of door bell. MACEY throws the rag doll into the box of toys and books then exits……returns with JIMMY.

Where the hell have you been?

JIMMY: Staffing problems.

MACEY: Boo hoo. I've just nearly had me flat wrecked. (*Pause.*) Well? Did yer bring it?

JIMMY hands her an envelope. MACEY counts the cash.

JIMMY: It's all there. (*She continues to count.*) I've set up a meet on Sunday. 2 o'clock at the bistro.

MACEY: What for?

JIMMY: So you can see the guy. Get to know him.

MACEY: I don't want to know him.

JIMMY: You've got to pass yourselves off as lovers, remember?… Remember?

MACEY: Yeah yeah. Lovers. I'll wear a big stupid grin on me face shall I?

MACEY puts the money in the ceramic jar. JIMMY takes out his wallet.

JIMMY: You got anything on? I've got an hour to kill.

MACEY: I haven't. I've got to pick me kids up from school.

JIMMY: Half an hour?

Little pause.

MACEY: Not a second over. And I get paid whether yer come or not. Bedroom's that way.

JIMMY exits. MACEY eats some beans from the saucepan. Lights down.

Scene Eight

Split Scene: CLIFF's bed sit / CHERYL's bed sit.

Darkness. The sound of bed springs creaking - a slow, steady, joyless rhythm. Lights up on CLIFF at his dresser, drinking, looking up (at the source of the sound). Lights down on CLIFF.

Lights up on CHERYL's bed sit. CHERYL is in bed, sheets pulled up to her neck. SAM is getting dressed. The birthday card is still on display.

SAM: Well Cheryl… I have to say…that was just fucking horrible. I mean it. The dullest ten minutes I've ever spent. I'd have had more fun sticking my dick in a milk bottle. (*Pause.*) This won't do, girl. I'm starting to feel cheated. And I do not like to feel cheated. (*Pause.*) Carry on like this, and we'll have to scrap our arrangement. I mean it. (*Pause.*) It's no wonder you've got no energy. Look at you…you look like a fucking Biafran.

CHERYL: …?

SAM: … Before your time. But you want to eat something for God's sake. Put some flesh back on those bones of yours.

Pause.

CHERYL: Did you bring me any food?

SAM: Yeah. As it happens. Out of the goodness of my heart.

SAM picks up a supermarket carrier bag, takes things out of it, flings them on the bed.

SAM: Here. Tin of Spam…corned dog…

CHERYL: I'm vegetarian.

SAM: Well that's not helping is it?

CHERYL: I don't like meat.

SAM: You're telling me. Tin of soup – chicken and mushroom…

CHERYL: Meat makes me sick.

SAM: Just eat the mushrooms then... (you're so fucking picky) ... packet of digestives...half a loaf...Pot Noodle... and some cheese I found in the back of the fridge. (*He sniffs the cheese, flings it on the bed.*) Well, don't say thanks or nothing. (*Pause. He picks up the card from the dresser.*) You ever going to take this card down?

CHERYL: Give me that...please.

SAM opens the card.

CHERYL: Please give me that.

SAM hands it back to her. He looks at his watch.

SAM: Right. I might as well pay a call on the inmates, collect some rent while I'm here. I'll see you next week. And I'd appreciate you putting some bloody effort into it... 'stead of lying there like a bleeding corpse... (I swear to Christ, it's like necrophilia what goes on in this room...) And would it kill you to smile once in a while?... Oh, and another thing, I'm not crazy about all that hair under your arms. Do something about it. Like two fucking gerbils under there. It's off-putting.

SAM exits. A moment. CHERYL reaches under her bed and pulls out her violin case. She clutches it to her breast. Lights slowly down...

And lights up on: CLIFF's bed sit.

SAM is fingering some bank notes, counting...

SAM: Here, you're ten pounds short.

CLIFF: That's correct.

SAM: Explain.

CLIFF: Roof. Toilet. Kitchen sink. Rats.

SAM: Rats? What fucking rats?

CLIFF: This place has rats.

SAM: Like shite it does.

CLIFF: There's droppings.

SAM: Where?

CLIFF: All over.

SAM: Show me.

CLIFF: I've cleaned them up.

SAM: Yeah right. Cough up, bollocks.

CLIFF: Droppings. *And* I've had them analyzed. Here… (*Gives him a letter.*) … Environmental Health. Bona fide rat droppings. Ergo, I'm withholding ten pounds per week rent until you sort out all the problems. We all are.

SAM: We?

CLIFF: The other tenants. I've organized a collective.

SAM: You taking the piss?

CLIFF: Everyone 'cept Cheryl who, because of her… circumstances, would rather not get involved. We have legitimate grievances Mr McDonald.

SAM: Listen. Faggot. Are you looking for trouble?

CLIFF: No. I'm looking for fairness. That's all. Equity. I know my rights.

Pause.

SAM: I knew you were going to give me grief. The moment you minced into this place. Freak.

CLIFF: Oh dear, is that the best you can do? Freak. Faggot. Mince. I'll be tossing and turning all night.

SAM: Look you. How would you like to find yourself out on the street?

CLIFF: How would you like to find yourself up in court?… Don't underestimate me, Mr McDonald. You see, I happen to have this lawyer acquaintance…and he'd just love to do a little pro bono on you.

SAM: Yeah. And I happen to have this huge spade who'd like to tear off your head and take a dump in your neck.

CLIFF: Marvin? Oh well, by all means, send Marvin round.

Pause. SAM steps closer towards CLIFF…raises his arm as if to strike CLIFF. CLIFF flinches. But SAM runs his hand through his own hair. Smiles. SAM starts to hum 'We'll Meet Again' as he exits. Little pause. CLIFF sighs with relief. His hand is shaking. Little pause. Sound of violin. CLIFF looks up.

Blackout.

The 'brick wall' descends. Underneath KEEP ENGLAND WITE! someone has sprayed: KEEP LIVERPOOL RED! (in red paint), and KEEP EVERTON BLUE! (in blue paint). This now forms the backdrop to the next scene…but first:

MBUSSO and SHPETIM perform a rendition of The Beatles' 'In My Life'. SHPETIM is technically very efficient. But MBUSSO – equally efficient – also plays with deep feeling. He's 'lost' in the melody. BEHROUZ enters and hands a bag of chips to SHPETIM. BEHROUZ and SHPETIM exit. MBUSSO plays on, alone, for several bars. He then props up his double bass against a wall and exits…

Scene Nine

Great Homer Street Market. Saturday Evening.

Market is packing away. SAMIR and SHPETIM sitting on crates. All the musical instruments are propped up against a wall. SHPETIM is eating from his bag of chips. SAMIR lights up a cigarette and watches him eat…

SAMIR: What is fascination with chip?

SHPETIM shrugs.

You have chip in Albania?

SHPETIM shrugs.

What is other thing in bag?

SHPETIM holds up a vinegar-soaked, battered fish.

Is fish?

SHPETIM shrugs.

Is insult to memory of fish to cook like that. (*Pause.*) You are quiet man Shpetim. Like Mbusso.

MOHAMMED enters carrying a plastic bag.

MOHAMMED: Is right what Behrouz say, wait till market close, is best for deal. Wait you see. Five pound. Is great deal. (*He takes a cheap gaudy shirt from the bag, holds it up.*) What you think?

SAMIR: Is…very…colourful, Mohammed.

MOHAMMED: Yes! Is big with colour! Is Versace. Man say is good make. Tom Cruise wear shirt like this. I wear for date with Macey. Tomorrow. You think she will like?

BEHROUZ enters carrying a plastic bag.

BEHROUZ: (*To MOHAMMED.*) *This* is shirt you buy? You buy sunglasses also?

MOHAMMED: Sunglasses?

BEHROUZ: You get Ray Bans for two quids. From man over there. You hurry you catch him.

MOHAMMED: I no need sunglasses. What you buy, Behrouz?

BEHROUZ takes out a Liverpool FC replica shirt.

BEHROUZ: Liverpool FC. Is wick-k-k-ed. Best team in world.

SAMIR: Very smart Behrouz. Where is sense? Wear red shirt and blue tribe beat you up.

BEHROUZ pulls out an Everton FC replica shirt.

BEHROUZ: Everton FC. Is wick-k-k-ed. Best team in world.

SAMIR: And red tribe beat you up.

BEHROUZ: I wear both at same time. I cheer for both team, everybody happy.

SAMIR: You are crazy boy, Behrouz.

BEHROUZ: Is girl on stall. She say same. She say 'you are off your cak-k-k-e'.

MOHAMMED: Cake?

BEHROUZ: Cak-k-k-e. Is expression. But pretty girl. Look, I buy firework also.

SAMIR: Why you buy firework?

BEHROUZ: We can have party. On roof. Food and drink. And firework.

SAMIR: Where Mbusso?

BEHROUZ: Where you think? He go to Kwik-k-k-ie. (*Gestures 'drinking'.*)

SAMIR: You tell him we work tonight?

BEHROUZ: Sure I tell him.

STELLA enters. She's eighteen, pretty, wearing a shell suit.

STELLA: (*To BEHROUZ.*) Hey! You! Yeah you…yer forgot yer change.

BEHROUZ: Change? (*She hands it over.*) Is only ten pence.

STELLA: So? It's *your* ten pence.

BEHROUZ: What I buy for ten pence?

STELLA: Get a tin of beans in the Kwikie for that.

BEHROUZ: Beans?

STELLA: Or tomatoes.

BEHROUZ: … OK.

STELLA: Or yer could make a phone call.

She hands him a slip of paper. He looks at it.

BEHROUZ: Who is…Stella?

STELLA: Who d'yer think soft lad?

BEHROUZ: Is you?

Little pause. STELLA groans and snatches back the paper.

STELLA: If yer not interested forget it.

BEHROUZ: (*Snatching back the paper…*) No. No. I have interest. Course I have interest. You are fit as fuck-k-k-k.

STELLA: Yer what?

BEHROUZ: Is right expression? I ask man about this. He say is compliment for girl.

A beat. STELLA smiles… BEHROUZ smiles.

STELLA: Don't waste yer ten pence.

STELLA leaves. BEHROUZ almost visibly swells with pride and self-satisfaction. MBUSSO enters, drinking from a can of lager and carrying the remains of a four pack.

SAMIR: Mbusso, my friend, is too early for drink, yes? Maybe I take and save for later?

SAMIR holds out his hand for the cans. MBUSSO gently shakes his head, collects his double bass and exits. The others follow.

BEHROUZ: Hey, Mohammed, look… (*Tosses the coin.*) Heads I win… (*Tosses the coin.*) … Tails I win.

Scene Ten

SAM's Office.

SAM and MARVIN sit at a table. SAM drinking whisky. He's also looking at his face in a hand mirror. MARVIN has a large plaster on the side of his face, and a bandage over one hand. Stacks of cash on the table. MARVIN is adding to it, making notes in a ledger. There is a leaflet protruding from the ledger.

MARVIN: 49 Croxteth Road: Flat 2…paid. Flat 3…paid.

SAM: Two big tower blocks, Marvin. Think about it.

MARVIN: Flat 4 paid and coughed half his arrears…says he'll have the rest in a fortnight.

SAM: Fourteen floors in each tower block. Four flats on each floor.

MARVIN: 86 Smithdown. Moonlight flit.

SAM: 56 flats per tower block! One hundred and twelve little gold mines!

MARVIN: What d'you want me to do?

SAM: A pound each Marvin! A hundred pence! For a whole tower block! I could have had them! Two years ago. I was offered them. But I said no. No fucking way. Look at them! Crumbling to pieces. Imagine the maintenance. What d'you take me for, a mug? (*He drinks…*) So I passed on the deal, Marvin. I passed. And I could be sitting on a mountain of gold right now. Two mountains. Twin glistening peaks. (*Pause.*) What?

MARVIN: 86 Smithdown.

SAM: What about it?

MARVIN: Moonlight flit. What d'you want me to do?

SAM: How much?

MARVIN: (*Checks ledger.*) Three hundred.

SAM: … Fuck it. Put an ad in the *Echo*.

SAM pours himself more whisky. MARVIN goes back to his book-keeping.

SAM: What about that bitch in Gambier Terrace? The mouthy one with the ugly sprogs.

MARVIN: … She settled.

SAM: All of it?

MARVIN: All of it.

SAM: About fucking time. She rubs me up that one. (Gob on her.)

MARVIN: 23 Lodge Lane. Both flats paid.

SAM: You know who bought them, don't you? Eh?

MARVIN: 56 Lodge Lane…paid…but still griping about the state of the roof.

SAM: Marvin. Stop that a minute. I'm trying to have a conversation here. You know who bought those two flats?

MARVIN: Which two flats?

SAM: Where the asylum seekers are living! Pay attention Marvin.

MARVIN: … Some foreign businessman wasn't it?

SAM: A Paki, Marvin. Some bloody Paki with inside information.

MARVIN: I heard he was from Iraq.

SAM: What?

MARVIN: Iraq. Iran. Syria. Somewhere round that way.

SAM: What's the difference. Whoever he is, he was tipped off. That's the point, Marvin. Boat loads of asylum seekers were getting shipped in. Each and every one of them paid for by the government. By our taxes, Marvin. Our taxes.

MARVIN: What you talking about? You don't pay tax.

SAM: Shut up. I've paid tax. In my time… Palms were greased. That's what I'm driving at. Cocks were sucked. The whole fucking system's corrupt.

MARVIN goes back to his book-keeping. SAM drinks and looks at himself in the mirror.

MARVIN: 23 Upper Parlie. Flat 1 paid. Flat 2 no answer. Flat 1 says Flat 2's on holiday.

SAM: Can I ask you something Marvin? Do you think I'm good looking?

MARVIN: … Eh?

SAM: You know. Handsome. Easy on the eye… All right, I'm not a kid anymore. But my face has got character. It's full of character… What d'you think?

MARVIN shrugs.

I'm clean. I always smell nice. This aftershave ain't cheap. And I wear good clobber. I drive a Merc for chrissake. I'm a fucking catch. (*Pause.*) If you was a bird d'you think you'd go for me?

MARVIN: I don't know what you're on about.

SAM: What I'm asking – would I repel you? (*Little pause. He sighs…*) If you was a bird, Marvin, if you was one of the opposite species, would the thought of having sex with me strike you as abhorrent?

MARVIN: Is this a trick question?

Pause.

SAM: I've got this bit of young stuff…

MARVIN: Oh yeah?

SAM: But I don't think she's keen.

MARVIN: No?

SAM: Her heart's not in it. (*Pause.*) Don't know why I'm so bothered, she's a shit shag.

MARVIN: So what you seeing her for then?

SAM: 'Cause she's young Marvin. And it's on a bloody plate. And when it's on a plate, you tuck in. (*Pause.*) No. I'm going to have to do something about the situation. I'm starting to lose my self-respect. (*Pause.*) Well, there's no way she's getting free lodging, she'll have to pay her way. (*Little pause.*) Do you know any pimps? (*Pause.*) How's it work? (*Pause.*) Come on, you must know some pimps.

MARVIN: Must I?

SAM: Well, don't you?

MARVIN: Have you got any idea how offensive that is? Yeah, my social circle's just full of pimps and whores and crack fiends.

SAM: Yeah yeah. All right. Don't get the hump. I didn't mean to insult your whole fucking race. I just thought…forget it. (*Jesus.*) You're a touchy bugger sometimes, Marvin. Got skin like bloody tissue paper. (*Pause.*) You having girl trouble or something?

MARVIN's mobile goes off. He answers it.

MARVIN: Hello?… Oh, hi. Yeah…yeah, I'm fine. How are you? Good… Yeah, my mum's fine, thanks for asking… Yeah, she does. She loves it… Well… She's never owned her own house before… I will…thanks… Yeah, he's here… just a minute. (*To SAM, handing the phone over.*) It's the missus.

SAM: (*Into phone.*) What?… How the hell should I know?… They're *your* bloody car keys Sheila. (*Sarcastically.*)… Try the drinks cabinet… Well, you'll just have to take a taxi then won't you?… Look… Christ… I'm doing the books, Sheila, I haven't got time for all this… Take a taxi, take a bus, walk for all I care… just don't go mental on the Am Ex. (*He snaps the phone shut and tosses it back to Marvin. Pause.*) What's she ringing your mobile for?

MARVIN shrugs. Pause. SAM sees the leaflet protruding from the ledger, takes it out, looks at it.

SAM: What's this all about?… Business Studies?

MARVIN: Thought I might do a correspondence course.

SAM: You?

MARVIN: Me.

SAM: What for?

MARVIN: Better myself.

SAM: (*Laughs.*)… Is this a wind up?

MARVIN: You don't think I'm going to spend my whole life in the muscle market?

SAM: … Oh, behave.

MARVIN: I'm serious. (*Bandage and plaster.*) I'm getting tired of this shit.

SAM: What, a couple of squatters get a bit frisky and you want a career change? Do me a favour. I thought you were happy in your work. Keeping the NHS busy.

MARVIN: I've got ambitions.

SAM: Work in an office? 15K a year? Get real, Marvin. (*Long pause. He takes a package from the desk drawer.*) Well, Mr Ambition, if you're not too busy doing your homework, I've got a job for you. Here. I want you to drop this off at the Stag and Hounds. Guy called Jason. You'll easy recognise him, he's an ugly little cunt with a hair lip.

MARVIN: (*Picks up the package.*) What is it?

SAM: Never mind what it is. He'll be there at 4 o'clock. Sat by the fruit machine. Shell suit and a baseball cap. He'll give you three hundred.

MARVIN: Is this what I think it is?

SAM: Depends what you think it is.

MARVIN: (*Pushes the package back.*) I don't think so. (*Little pause.*) D'you know how often I get pulled over by the bizzies? That's all I need, a bloody gun in the car.

Pause.

SAM: Don't I pay you enough, Marvin?

MARVIN: I've got no complaints about my wages.

SAM: Good. I was starting to sense a lack of appreciation for my generosity.

He pushes the package back towards MARVIN who, in turn, pushes it back towards SAM. Pause.

SAM: Does your mother like living in that nice new bungalow of hers?

Little pause. He pushes the package towards MARVIN who, in turn, pushes it back towards SAM.

MARVIN: Not on the job description.

SAM: What fucking job description? (*Long pause.*) What's got into you lately, Marvin? Eh? Your moods are up and down like a who-er's drawers… suddenly you've got 'ambitions'… and now these horrible little scruples. What's going on? (*Pause.*) I've never known such a contrary fucking spade in all my life.

Pause.

MARVIN: You know, I'd appreciate it if you didn't keep calling me a spade.

SAM: It's a term of endearment.

Long pause. SAM lights up a cigarette.

MARVIN: What you getting involved in this racket for anyway?

SAM: Have you learnt nothing while you've been working for me?

MARVIN: Oh. Right. This your idea of 'diversification', is it?

SAM: Fingers and pies, Marvin. Fingers and pies.

MARVIN: These things kill people.

SAM: So do cigarettes. Grow up. It's a free world.

MARVIN: For who?

SAM: For everyone. I don't discriminate.

MARVIN: Right. Right. And some stupid kid gets involved in a petty dispute and decides to settle it with one of these.

SAM: And if not one of these, then a knife or a baseball bat. What's the fucking difference? If he didn't get it from me he'd get it from someone else… Anyway, one less punk on the streets, it's practically a community service. They should give me a bloody medal.

SAM finishes his drink, picks up the gun, stands.

Right. I'll go and drop this off myself, shall I?

Little pause. SAM exits. MARVIN continues with his book-keeping.

Blackout. SOUND of rain. Live rendition of 'Something' by The Beatles starts up…

Scene Eleven

Split Scene: The Bistro and The Kitchen.

The Bistro.

THE TROUBADOURS, at the back, playing 'Something'. They look a bit wet and bedraggled. As does… MOHAMMED who is sat at a table with MACEY. He presents her with a small bunch of flowers. She rolls her eyes and puts the flowers on the table. MOHAMMED drinks from his bottle of water. He can't take his eyes off MACEY. She drinks from a bottle of beer. She glances back at THE TROUBADOURS…

MOHAMMED: Is pretty song, no?… Pretty like you.

MACEY smiles weakly at the compliment. Pause.

MOHAMMED: My father, he was musician. He play tenbur.

MACEY: Oh yeah? What's one of them?

MOHAMMED: Tenbur? Is…is like, what you say…? (*Mimes a wind instrument.*)

MACEY: Flute.

MOHAMMED: Guitar.

MACEY: Eh?

MOHAMMED: … Is joke. (*Pause.*) Woman in Liverpool, she like joke, yes?

MACEY: Depends.

MOHAMMED: I told she like joke. (*He looks at BEHROUZ.*) Make Liverpool woman laugh, everything hunky dokey.

MACEY: *Dory.*

MOHAMMED: Please?… And Liverpool woman, she like song by Beatle. Yes?

MACEY: I prefer the Wombles.

MOHAMMED: … Wombles? Is musician from Liverpool?

MACEY: Yeah. They're from the Dingle.

MOHAMMED: Wombles from the Dingle. (*He looks across at The TROUBADOURS.*) You want I should ask? They play any song you like. Any song. (*Long pause.*) You like shirt?

MACEY: What?

JIMMY enters with two plates of food.

What's with the band, 'Mister Jimmy'?

JIMMY: Nothing to do with me.

MACEY: What's with the flowers, Mister Jimmy?

JIMMY: Ditto.

MACEY: What's with the glint in his eye and the big stupid grin, Mister Jimmy?

JIMMY: Go easy.

MACEY: He's giving me the creeps.

MOHAMMED: (*The food.*) Oh…is good, Mister Jimmy. Is good big smell. What is?

JIMMY: Tanjia Marrakchia.

MOHAMMED: Please?

JIMMY: It's Moroccan.

MOHAMMED: Moroccan. What go in?

JIMMY: Lamb. Garlic. Lemon. Cumin. Saffron.

MACEY: Got any ketchup? (*Beat. Smiles.*) Joke.

MOHAMMED laughs even though he doesn't get the joke.

MOHAMMED: Macey like joke, yes? I like joke. Is thing we have in common.

JIMMY: Enjoy.

MOHAMMED picks up his plate and hands it back to JIMMY.

MOHAMMED: Mister Jimmy…thank you. Many thank you. Maybe Mohammed enjoy later… Is Ramadan. I no eat till sky is black. Thank you.

JIMMY: Ramadan? But I've just spent… Why didn't you say something?

MOHAMMED: Mister Jimmy is very kind. Is no problem. I watch Macey eat.

JIMMY is about to exit with the plate when BEHROUZ hurries over…

BEHROUZ: Is OK, mate. I will eat. No worries, mate… Cheers mate. Nice one. Is Scouse?

JIMMY: No, it's Tanj… yeah, it's Scouse.

JIMMY exits. BEHROUZ stares at MACEY.

MACEY: What are *you* gawping at?

BEHROUZ rejoins THE TROUBADOURS. Lights down.

Lights up on: The Kitchen.

CLIFF is sat on a stool drinking a mug of tea. JIMMY is cleaning some dishes.

CLIFF: … Go on.

JIMMY: No.

CLIFF: Just come round to the house.

JIMMY: I said no.

CLIFF: I'll cook a meal or something… Just see her.

JIMMY: For the last time, no!

CLIFF: … Please… Pretty please? (*Little pause.*) I was thinking –

JIMMY: Cliff, save your breath, 'cause I'm not getting involved in this.

Little pause.

CLIFF: Maybe you could give her a job or something.

JIMMY: Grow up.

CLIFF: Just part-time. Few hours a week. I could walk her here, walk her back home. What d'you say? (*Pause.*) Might do wonders for her self-esteem. (*Pause.*) You know how I think she's paying her rent don't you?

JIMMY: You don't know that for certain.

CLIFF: Feminine intuition.

JIMMY: Well, it's *her* choice. And it's none of my business. Actually, I don't see that it's any of yours either… Just leave the girl alone if she wants to be left alone.

CLIFF: Christ you're cold.

JIMMY: I have enough trouble getting through my own life.

CLIFF puts his head against JIMMY's chest.

What are you doing?

CLIFF: Sshhh… Well, something's ticking away in there. Fuck knows what it could be. You must've swallowed a watch or something. (*Long pause.*) You know why you keep getting migraines, don't you? It's all this…negative energy… swirling around inside you. (*Little pause.*) You need your aura cleansing.

JIMMY: Oh shut up. You tart.

Pause. MOHAMMED enters with the bunch of flowers.

MOHAMMED: Mister Jimmy… Excuse… Forgive.

JIMMY: What is it Mohammed?

MOHAMMED: Macey. She go.

JIMMY: Go where?

MOHAMMED: She have phone call, say she must go work.

JIMMY: Well, there's nothing I can do about that.

MOHAMMED: Sunday is day for rest in this country. Yes?

CLIFF: That's rather an old fashioned notion.

MOHAMMED: You no tell me Macey work.

JIMMY: It's none of your business whether she works or not.

MOHAMMED: No. Is OK Mister Jimmy. Is fine she work… She forget flower. I give for you.

JIMMY: I don't want them.

CLIFF: Give them here. Put them anywhere near him they'll die of toxic poisoning. I'll put them in some glasses.

CLIFF exits.

MOHAMMED: Mister Jimmy… Macey, she is very pretty. She make my heart go… (*Gestures 'faster'.*) You know how to pick pretty girl. Thank you. Thank you, Mister Jimmy.

JIMMY: Don't go overboard Mohammed, it's just business, remember?

Pause.

MOHAMMED: I think she really like me. You think she really like me? I think I make Macey heart go… (*Gestures 'faster'.*) When we marry, Mister Jimmy?

JIMMY: Soon as I can sort out the licence.

MOHAMMED: I want you to be man who is best… Is thing you have, yes? Is custom here? Best Man? Is good custom. (*Pause.*) You want I should help Mister Jimmy? I clean plate for you.

JIMMY: There's no need.

MOHAMMED: Is no problem. (*Pause.*) Hey, Mister Jimmy, my friends? They all jealous, I think.

Lights down on kitchen. Lights up on: The Bistro.

CLIFF is sat at a table, arranging the flowers into small glasses. THE TROUBADOURS are sat round the table previously occupied by MOHAMMED and MACEY. BEHROUZ is finishing off what's left of his meal; SHPETIM is eating from the plate of food Macey left. MBUSSO is drinking from the bottle of beer. (NB. During this beat of the scene, SAMIR and

BEHROUZ occasionally speak in perfect RP English, to signify they are, in fact, speaking in their native tongue of Farsi.)

SAMIR: (*RP.*) What on earth do you mean?

BEHROUZ: Which part of that sentence could you not understand?

SAMIR: Are you saying…

BEHROUZ: (*To CLIFF, pidgin English:*) Hey mate…excuse mate…you have bread? Bread for juice?

CLIFF: Would you like white or brown?

BEHROUZ: Is all same for me.

CLIFF: Butter?

BEHROUZ: Butter is good. Cheers mate.

CLIFF exits…

SAMIR: Are you telling me this girl's a prostitute? This girl here?

BEHROUZ: Did you see any other girl?

Little pause.

SAMIR: Are you certain of this?

BEHROUZ: Absolutely certain.

Little pause.

SAMIR: How do you know she is a prostitute?… What makes you so sure, Behrouz?

BEHROUZ: Isn't it obvious?

SAMIR: Not to me.

BEHROUZ: Perhaps you need your eyes testing.

SAMIR: She dresses no different to other young women. (*Little pause.*) Have you been spending time with prostitutes?… Behrouz?

BEHROUZ: I've seen this girl on the streets.

SAMIR: Tell me you haven't been with prostitutes… Show me your vouchers.

BEHROUZ: Samir, there's something I feel you need reminding of: you are not my father. OK? Can we at least agree on that?… Mohammed's in for big surprise I think.

SAMIR: You say nothing to Mohammed.

BEHROUZ: Why not? If he's going to marry a prostitute, don't you think he has the right to know?

SAMIR: It's not important for him to know. It's simply a business arrangement. That's all. There's no reason to destroy his hopes.

BEHROUZ: Or his illusions?… Let me ask you something, Samir: why do you always look out for Mohammed? You invite him to join the band. He can barely whistle a good tune. He contributes nothing and yet we split the takings five ways.

SAMIR: There's a worrying streak of avarice in you, Behrouz.

CLIFF approaches, puts the bread and butter on the table.

BEHROUZ: You think I'm greedy because I want what's rightfully mine? I have to send money home. And all this time, he's been sleeping on, what, five thousand pounds?

CLIFF: … I enjoyed listening to your music earlier.

BEHROUZ: Did you know he had all that money?… Did you?

They acknowledge CLIFF's presence for the first time (and now revert back to their familiar pidgin English).

CLIFF: Sorry, I don't mean to intrude…

SAMIR: Yes?

CLIFF: That's a beautiful language. What is that?

SAMIR: Is Farsi.

CLIFF: Farsi.

SAMIR: We are from Iran.

CLIFF: … I just wanted to tell you how much I enjoyed your music.

SAMIR: Thank you.

CLIFF: I've seen you all on the streets before. In fact, I even followed you through the town once, just to listen to you. It was just like the pied piper. Do you fellas perform at functions at all?

SAMIR: What is function?

CLIFF: Weddings? I have a friend who's getting married soon. Well, it's not an official wedding. More of a ceremony really. But with all the trimmings.

SAMIR: Is one of Mister Jimmy's weddings?

CLIFF: (*Confused.*) Jimmy? No. It's got nothing to do with Jimmy.

BEHROUZ: (*To SAMIR, RP.*) Maybe Jimmy has a little sideline in homosexual relationships. That Chinese guy… across the landing? The one who always smells of lavender. He might be interested. What do you think? (*To CLIFF, pidgin.*) How much Mister Jimmy pay for marriage to you?

CLIFF: Excuse me?

BEHROUZ: Mister Jimmy. He what you call…? What is word? He pimp. Yes?

SAMIR: Stop Behrouz.

BEHROUZ: How much for marriage?

SAMIR: (*To CLIFF.*) Please ignore.

Pause.

CLIFF: Let me get this straight… Are you…? Let me see if I'm understanding you correctly. Are you telling me that Jimmy… 'Mister Jimmy'…he's arranging marriages for you people? Is that what you're saying?

SAMIR: Is just business.

CLIFF: But you *pay* him?

SAMIR: He find girl. Is business.

JIMMY enters with a plate of food and a glass of water. He sits alone at a table. CLIFF watches him, barely able to conceal his contempt. He goes over to JIMMY's table, stares down at him…

JIMMY: Oh, what is it now?… Spit it out… *What?*

CLIFF picks up JIMMY's water and throws it in his face.

JIMMY: For the love of…! What the hell was *that* for?!

CLIFF: …You disgust me.

JIMMY: What else is new?

CLIFF: You're taking money from these people?… Well?

JIMMY dries himself off, resumes eating…

CLIFF: You're so far beneath contempt I wouldn't even know where to begin digging… Don't just sit there eating your fucking dinner!

JIMMY: Stay out of it, Cliff.

JIMMY continues to eat. CLIFF takes the salt-cellar, removes the lid, and throws the salt all over JIMMY's meal. Pause.

JIMMY: I'm providing a service. All right? *They* come to *me.*

CLIFF: Oh aye. Sure. Sure they do. Got an advert in the *Yellow Pages* have you?

JIMMY: Nobody's twisting their arms.

CLIFF: They're bloody asylum seekers, Jimmy! They haven't got a pot to piss in.

JIMMY: You don't know what you're talking about. For your information –

CLIFF: They're living on bloody food vouchers for God's sake.

JIMMY: They're not *all* living on food vouchers. Some of them –

CLIFF: What is it with you? Eh? What? Are you totally *a*moral?

JIMMY: Hey, I didn't create this situation. OK?

CLIFF: No. You're just trying to profit from it.

JIMMY: Nobody's exploiting them. They get what they want. I get what I want. Everybody's happy.

CLIFF: Happy. *Happy!* You don't know the meaning of the word. You miserable specimen. (*Little pause.*) You know, if I was any good at fighting I'd beat the crap out of you right now. I would.

MARVIN enters, goes to CLIFF who is surprised to see him.

MARVIN: You got a minute?… I need to talk to you… I need to talk to you now.

CLIFF: OK. But first, do me a favour – give him a thump would you?

MARVIN: What?!

CLIFF: Go on. Just hit him. Just the once. Right in his big thick head.

MARVIN: Look, don't fuck about, I'm in a hurry. I've got to be some place.

They go off to one side.

CLIFF: (*The plaster, bandage:*) What happened to you?

MARVIN: (*Ignoring him.*) Listen. The Irish girl.

CLIFF: … Cheryl. Yeah. What about her?

MARVIN: You'd better tell her to get her shit together.

CLIFF: I would if I knew what that meant.

MARVIN: It means you'd better get her some help. Quick. Get her to the doctor. Do something.

CLIFF: I'm trying, I'm trying.

MARVIN: Well, try harder.

CLIFF: What's this all about?

MARVIN: I haven't got time to go into all the details, but it's important you –

MARVIN's mobile phone goes off. He checks the caller's name, sighs.

I'm on my way… I'm stuck in traffic…should be there in about ten… Right… Yeah… OK. (*To CLIFF.*) I've got to go.

CLIFF: Hang on. Is that it? I need something more than that.

MARVIN: I haven't got time. Just have a word with her.

CLIFF: A word. Right. And which particular word would you recommend?

MARVIN: I'm trying to do you a favour.

CLIFF: … Yeah. I know. (*Little pause.*) Listen, I don't suppose there's any chance of you…?

MARVIN: I've really got to go.

MARVIN exits. MOHAMMED enters from the kitchen, a towel in his hands.

MOHAMMED: Is all clean Mister Jimmy. Clean and dry and put away.

CLIFF: What's this, slave labour?

MOHAMMED: Is more to do, Mister Jimmy? You want I should clean floor?

CLIFF: Is he paying you? Then no, he doesn't want you should clean floor. Take my advice and don't do anything for him…he'll have the shirt off your back before you know it.

MOHAMMED: Is nice shirt. You want, Mister Jimmy? Is yours you want.

JIMMY: You'd best go now Mohammed. Go on. I'll be in touch… Go on.

MOHAMMED hands the towel to JIMMY then leaves with THE TROUBADOURS. CLIFF glares at JIMMY then exits to the kitchen. JIMMY lights up a cigarette, plays with the food on his plate, pushes the plate away.

Scene Twelve

The garden. Morning.

Birdsong. Lights up on CHERYL and CLIFF. He's helping her take her first tentative steps outside. CHERYL is wearing a baseball cap, the peak pulled down as far as it will go. She has her head down, humming a tune to herself.

CLIFF: That's it…that's it…you're doing fine, Cheryl… you're doing brilliantly… Look at you!… I'm so proud of you!… Again?

CHERYL: No.

CLIFF: Once more around the garden?

CHERYL: I want to go in.

CLIFF: OK. In a minute. Let's just pause for a moment…

CHERYL: I want to go back inside.

CLIFF: Just a – come here, Cheryl…just a second or two… I promise… I promise… let's just take a moment…to breathe in this crisp morning air…a slow deep breath… let's fill up our lungs…come on Cheryl…a slow, deep… that's it…take in all that lovely oxygen…and hold your breath for ten seconds…… and…let it out…slowly… slowly now…isn't that refreshing? Hmmm? Listen…listen to the birds. Isn't that beautiful? Look at the sky. Look, Cheryl… Isn't that just the perfect shade of blue? I've got a frock that colour. It always cheers me up… And there's the moon. See? The morning moon. Couldn't sleep. (*Pause.*) See? There's nothing to be afraid of.

Little pause. Suddenly a banger is thrown into the garden. CHERYL screams and runs back into the house. Sound of scallies laughing, running away.

CLIFF: BASTARDS! YOU LITTLE, SODDING BASTARDS!

Scene Thirteen

Street. MACEY's Flat. Early hours of the morning.

MOHAMMED and TROUBADOURS enter. They are carrying their instruments. It's cold. MBUSSO drinks from a half bottle of whisky. There is a bench to one side.

MOHAMMED: This is house.

SAMIR: Are you sure you want do this Mohammed? Is very late.

BEHROUZ: Is very early. And cold as fuck-k-k.

MOHAMMED: Macey work long shift at factory. This will please I think.

BEHROUZ: Is not called factory Mohammed, is called –

BEHROUZ silenced by a look from SAMIR.

Why you do this, Samir? Eh? You crazy as him!

MOHAMMED: Work of shift is bad. Make people work bad time. (*He takes a crumpled piece of paper from his pocket.*) I have word of song. Am ready, Samir.

SAMIR: Mohammed…my friend… I have question: you sure Macey like *this* song?

MOHAMMED: She say she like musician.

SAMIR: But is not song for romance I think.

MOHAMMED: Is only song I find. Is OK, Samir. Is hunky dory.

SAMIR shrugs. He plays a fancy intro…and BEHROUZ and MBUSSO and SHPETIM soon join in.

(*Singing.*) 'Underground, overground, wombling free,
The Wombles of Wimbledon Common are we
Making good use of the things that we find
Things that the everyday folks leave behind

Uncle Bulgaria, he can remember the days
When he wasn't behind the times
With his map of the world
Pick up the papers and take 'em to Tobermory…
Wombles are organized, work as a team
Wombles are tidy and Wombles are clean…'

Lights on in MACEY's flat…

(*Singing.*) 'Underground, overground, wombling free,
The Wombles of Wimbledon Common are we…'

Bedroom lights begin to flick on along the street… MACEY appears at one window, sleepy and confused. TROUBADOURS gradually stop playing.

MACEY: What the ..!!! What's going on down there?

MOHAMMED: Hello Macey!

MACEY: Who is that?… *Mohammed?!* Is that you? Jesus suffering Christ!

MOHAMMED: How are you?

MACEY: What the hell are yer doing down there yer mad fucker!

MOHAMMED: Is song for you Macey.

MACEY: D'yer know what frigging time it is?

MOHAMMED: Is song for cheer you up.

MOHAMMED signals SAMIR to play on.

(*Singing.*) 'Underground, overground, wombling free,
The Wombles of Wimbledon Common are we…'

MACEY: Oy! Knock it off. Yer soft get. Yer gonna wake me kids up. Wait there. Christ.

MACEY disappears from the window.

MOHAMMED: What she say? Kids?

BEHROUZ: Oh, she big cheer up, Mohammed. She have great big smile.

MOHAMMED: Kids is children, yes?

BEHROUZ: Is not goat.

MOHAMMED: Mister Jimmy no say Macey have children.

BEHROUZ: Mister Jimmy no say many thing.

MOHAMMED: … What you mean?

SAMIR: I think is mistake come here Mohammed. Come my friend. We go. Is late.

MACEY joins them on the street.

MACEY: What d'yer think yer playing at yer daft loon?

MOHAMMED: Hello Macey! How beautiful you look!

MACEY: Knock it off… What are yer doing here? Who gave yer me address?

MOHAMMED: Mister Jimmy. I say I want write you letter.

MACEY: … So. What d'yer want? Why've you come?

MOHAMMED: To see you. Is all. And to sing song for you. Is romantic, no?

MACEY: Yer taking the piss, right?

MOHAMMED: Mohammed heart is full of romance.

MACEY: Mohammed heart is full of crap.

MOHAMMED: You no like song?

MACEY: No.

MOHAMMED: But you like Womble. Yes? You say you like Womble.

MACEY: (Jesus.) I was just being…

MOHAMMED: I spend all day to practice. To learn word of song. Song is for you Macey. Is for make you smile.

She smiles in spite of herself, half laughs.

See! Song work. Song work like magic.

MACEY: God, yer not plumb are yer?

MOHAMMED: Plumb? What is plumb?

MACEY: Never mind. (*Little pause.*) Yer haven't got a fag on yer, have yer?

MOHAMMED: Fag?

MACEY: Ciggie. Cigarette.

MOHAMMED: I no smoke.

MOHAMMED turns to THE TROUBADOURS. BEHROUZ offers MACEY a cigarette, lights it for her.

MACEY: Come here Mo…

MACEY walks him to the bench.

MOHAMMED: You want coat? Is cold.

MACEY: No…

MOHAMMED takes off his coat anyway and drapes it over her shoulders…

There's no chance of *you* getting run over with that shirt on.

MOHAMMED: You like?

MACEY: Listen love. I know yer mean well. But we've really got to get something straight…

MOHAMMED: You have beauty like moon. Like stars in sky.

MACEY: Stop it. You're gonna make me puke.

MOHAMMED: Puke? What is puke?

MACEY: Look Mo –

MOHAMMED: -hammed. Is -hammed on the end.

MACEY: Did Jimmy explain all this to yer?… Did he?

MOHAMMED: Mister Jimmy tell me everything.

MACEY: So, yer do know what this is all about. Don't yer?

MOHAMMED: Is about love.

MACEY: No.

MOHAMMED: Is about… kismet.

MACEY: No.

MOHAMMED: Is about will of Allah.

MACEY: No. It's not. It's not about the will of Allah. It's not about love. It's not about kismet. It's not about any of those things. It's just business. It… it's just a transaction. That's all. Nothing more than that. (*Pause.*) Yer do understand, don't yer?

MOHAMMED: Man and woman. Together. Is gift. Gift from Allah. Man find woman, is blessing. Woman is light. Woman help show you way. Man with woman, no more darkness. (*Pause.*) This is word of father. (*Pause.*) Father have music in heart. And poetry. His heart big…big with wisdom. (*Beat.*) Great wisdom. (*Pause.*) Man with woman, no more darkness. Is lesson for life. One day I give wisdom to my son. (*Pause.*) You have children Macey?

MACEY: … What?

MOHAMMED: Kids? Children? Is what you say? Is what I hear?

MACEY: Yes I've got kids. What's it got to do with you?

MOHAMMED: Mister Jimmy no say you have children.

MACEY: Well, it's none of Jimmy's business. And it's none of yours either.

MOHAMMED: Where is father?

MACEY: Look. I think yer'd better go.

MOHAMMED: Is father dead? Is why Macey alone, yes? Is why Macey need husband?

MACEY: I don't *need* anyone. (*To the TROUBADOURS.*) Oy. Take him home will yer.

MOHAMMED: Is OK Macey. Is OK you have children. Mohammed like children.

SAMIR: Come Mohammed.

MOHAMMED: Mohammed would like see children.

MACEY: Take him home now. OK? Now. And don't come here again. Got it? None of yers. Don't ever come here again.

MACEY exits. Pause.

SAMIR: Come Mohammed. We go.

MOHAMMED: Is will of Allah. Mohammed be husband and father at same time.

TROUBADOURS and MOHAMMED wander off. BEHROUZ plays and sings 'Can't Buy Me Love' by The Beatles.

End of Act One.

ACT TWO

Scene Fourteen

A Street. Afternoon.

Darkness. A bass guitar. An infectious driving beat. Lights up on MBUSSO playing his double bass. He looks impatient, looks around him for the other band members... SHPETIM enters, holding his guitar. He slips into the song. Then... BEHROUZ enters through the auditorium, guitar slung over his shoulder, eating a Big Mac. He greets various members of the audience with:

BEHROUZ: Alright La!... How's it goin' wack?... Lookin' great der gerl!... Wick-k-ked... Sound as a pound... Later, yeah? Later.

And, with his mouth full of burger, he too slips into the song, which should now be recognizable as The Beatles' 'Get Back'. Finally... SAMIR enters, playing his accordion, and THE TROUBADOURS are into the song proper. MOHAMMED comes through the auditorium, holding his tambourine, seeking donations from the audience. Half way through the song a POLICEMAN enters, stands and watches. He's followed by an IMMIGRATION OFFICER holding an official document. They wait a short while before approaching SHPETIM. The IMMIGRATION OFFICER shows the document to SHPETIM. Then the POLICEMAN handcuffs SHPETIM and leads him away. The song peters out during this... MOHAMMED and remaining TROUBADOURS are left despondent. They exit.

Scene Fifteen

The Kitchen. Afternoon.

CLIFF is cutting CHERYL's hair...

CLIFF: ... Did you hear what I said?

CHERYL: There's nothing wrong with my ears.

CLIFF: … And?

CHERYL: I don't want to go for a walk round the block.

CLIFF: Might do you good.

CHERYL: No it won't.

CLIFF: Bit of fresh air.

CHERYL: I've got all the air I want in here.

Pause.

CLIFF: It's a beautiful day.

CHERYL: I don't care.

Pause.

CLIFF: Sun is shining. Autumn leaves. Trees in Sevvy Park are just stunning now.

CHERYL: You can forget the feckin' park… And I'm not going round the block with you either. So you can give yer tongue a rest… There's nothing out there for me… (Feckin' fireworks!)

Pause.

CLIFF: I thought you did brilliantly the other day. (*Pause.*) We really should try and build on that. (*Pause.*) I've got this friend who's training to be a counsellor. (*Pause.*) He's very good on depression. (*Pause.*) How would you like to talk to him?

CHERYL: I *wouldn't* like to talk to him! I don't want to talk to *any*one.

CLIFF: He's a really nice guy. Very sensitive.

CHERYL: (*Turning on him.*) Look, I said yer could cut me hair, I didn't say yer could badger me about going out and talking to yer friends.

Long pause.

CLIFF: You've got lovely thick hair, Cheryl. Really. You should come down to the college, be a model. I mean…

sorry…nothing. Slip of the tongue. (*Pause.*) Beautiful texture. Full bodied. Very Maureen O'Hara.

CHERYL: Who?

CLIFF: Actress?… *The Quiet Man?* (*A poor John Wayne impression.*) 'There'll be no chains on our marriage Mary Kate Danaher.'

CHERYL: She had a deep voice.

CLIFF: No! That was John Wayne. Silly… I'm better at women. (*A passable Bette Davis:*) 'Oh Jerry, don't let's ask for the moon: we have the stars.' (*Beat.*) Well?

CHERYL: Haven't a clue.

CLIFF: Bette Davis.

Little pause.

CHERYL: Yer like yer films don't yer? I hear yer playing yer videos all the time.

CLIFF: I like to lose myself. It's not healthy really…avoiding the real world, just so I can pretend to be Vivien Leigh for a couple of hours…or Judy…or Liza…or –

CLIFF suddenly screams…as a large brown RAT scurries across the stage.

CHERYL: … What?!

CLIFF: A RAT!

CHERYL: A rat?

CLIFF: (*Climbing on to the table.*) A BIG BROWN HAIRY FUCKING RAT!

CHERYL: (*Climbing onto the table.*) Where?! Where?!

CLIFF: It went that way!… Over there! Towards the back door!

CHERYL: … Are yer sure?

CLIFF: Didn't you see it?

CHERYL: No.

CLIFF: It was the size of a fucking dog!

Pause.

CHERYL: Jesus, yer scared the life out of me. (*Pause.*) What are we going to do?

CLIFF: I'll be fucked if I'm getting off this table while that thing's roaming around.

Pause.

CHERYL: We can't stay up here forever.

Pause. JIMMY enters from the hall, looks at the two of them on the table…

CLIFF: Jimmy.

JIMMY: … The door was open… What's going on?

CLIFF: A rat… A *rat!*… A big brown… It just came through the kitchen.

CHERYL: … It went that way.

JIMMY goes and looks…

JIMMY: I can't see anything.

CLIFF: Course you can't. The sneaky little fuckers can hide anywhere.

JIMMY goes to the table, holds out his hand, towards CHERYL. Instead, CLIFF takes JIMMY's hand and steps down from the table. Beat. JIMMY holds out his hand, and helps CHERYL down.

What d'you want anyway? What are you doing here? (*Little pause.*) Well?

JIMMY: What?… Oh. Diane quit on me.

CLIFF: I'm not surprised.

JIMMY: What's that supposed to mean?

CLIFF: Can't be any fun working for you. Being black… It's a wonder you didn't ship her off to America to work in the cotton fields.

Pause.

JIMMY: I need a waiter. I was wondering if you knew anyone who's looking for a job. (*Little pause.*) Well. Do you?

CLIFF: Off the top of my head?… Erm…let me see now. Hmmm…

CLIFF nods that JIMMY should ask CHERYL.

JIMMY: How about you?

CHERYL: … Me?

JIMMY: Yeah.

CHERYL: Wait tables?

JIMMY: You're a student aren't you?

CHERYL: No.

JIMMY: Oh. I thought you were a student.

CHERYL: What made yer think I was a student?

JIMMY: I don't know. You look like one. I suppose.

CLIFF: Cheryl's sort of taking a gap year right now.

Little pause.

JIMMY: It's just a few hours a week. What d'you say?

CHERYL: No thanks.

JIMMY: You'd be helping me out. And the money's not bad.

CHERYL: I don't need a job.

CLIFF: I could walk you there. Walk you home again.

CHERYL: Yer starting to get on my nerves, Cliff. Really.

CHERYL exits…

JIMMY: Well, that was a waste of time.

CLIFF: But you came. (*Little pause.*) Why d'you change your mind?

JIMMY: I need a waitress.

CLIFF: The real reason.

JIMMY: I need a waitress. Don't go romanticising.

CLIFF: Wait. Don't leave. Try again.

JIMMY: What?

CLIFF: Don't just throw in the towel.

JIMMY: You heard the girl. She doesn't want the job.

CLIFF: Quitter.

JIMMY: God almighty. What more d'you want me to do
Cliff? Really?

CLIFF: Stay for dinner. (*Little pause.*) I'm cooking dinner. I'll
set an extra place.

*Pause. JIMMY sighs, shrugs 'OK' and sits down. CLIFF exits.
Pause. A second rat scurries across the stage. JIMMY stands up,
alarmed.*

Scene Sixteen

Back room of a pub. Night.

*SAM, MARVIN and MOHAMMED. MARVIN sitting off to one side,
reading a leaflet.*

SAM: (*To MOHAMMED.*)… OK. Repeat.

MOHAMMED: Please?

SAM: Say what I've just said to you.

MOHAMMED: Re…peat?

SAM: Not that. *Every*thing I've just said to you… Your *job.*

MOHAMMED: Job. Yes. Job. OK Mister Sam. I bring glass
from table. I wash glass. I dry glass. I put glass on shelf. I
clean table. Tray for cigarette. I brush floor. Take out
rubbish. Take empty bottle into yard

SAM: … And?

MOHAMMED: … Please?

SAM: Good grief. And what else?… *Toilet?*

MOHAMMED: Oh! Yes. Yes. Toilet Mister Sam. I no forget. I clean toilet. Toilet for man. Toilet for woman.

SAM: I don't want no puke and shit smelling up the place.

MOHAMMED: I make very clean, Mister Sam. You no worry.

SAM: I've had complaints.

MOHAMMED: Mohammed is good for work.

SAM: One pound fifty an hour. OK?

MOHAMMED: Okey dokey.

SAM: It's minimum wage so no griping.

MOHAMMED: I work many hour Mister Sam. I have wife and family soon. I have three child. Next time, I bring picture, show you.

SAM: Lovely.

MOHAMMED: I work hard Mister Sam.

SAM: See that you do.

MOHAMMED: You no worry. I work like nigger.

SAM: … What did you say?

MOHAMMED: … I work like nigger.

A look between SAM and MARVIN.

Is thing I hear. Is work hard, yes? I have friend, doctor, who work in restaurant, clean dish. Boss man say, 'You very good. You work like nigger.' I work hard too. I no let you down Mister Sam.

Little pause. SAM looks conspicuously at his watch.

SAM: Go. To. Work.

MOHAMMED: Work. Yes. Thank you Mister Sam. Many thank you. I go now. I work for you.

MOHAMMED exits.

SAM: Keen as mustard. That's what I like to see. Makes a change from the work-shy retards I usually get lumbered with.

MARVIN: (*Holds up the leaflet.*) I found this in the filing cabinet... British Patriotic Front?

SAM: ... Take it easy, it's not what you think.

MARVIN: ... Membership form?

SAM: Marvin. Don't go getting your bollocks all knotted... It's just someone I'm doing business with.

Pause.

MARVIN: Someone you're doing business with wants you to join the BPF?

SAM: It's just for show. You know, Captains of Industry. That sort of thing. Raises their profile. (*Little pause.*) It's just business, Marvin. That's all. Contacts. Networking. (*Pause.*) It's just like joining the Masons.

Little pause.

MARVIN: The Jews weren't driven out of Germany by the Masons. Six million Jews weren't –

SAM: Marvin, for fuck's sake, don't go making a big deal out of it.

Pause. They stare at each other.

MARVIN: You don't think fascism's a big deal? (*Pause.*) This turns my stomach.

SAM: You've got nothing to fear from these pricks, they're a bunch of losers.

MARVIN: Easy said when you're white.

Long pause. SAM pours himself a whisky.

SAM: I'm beginning to sense a shift in our relationship, Marvin. Lately, a little...chagrin seems to have crept into your demeanour.

MARVIN: (*Correcting Sam's pronunciation:*) Chagrin.

SAM: …What?

MARVIN: It's pronounced chagrin.

SAM: … Watch it. (*Pause.*) I think it's about time you and I had a little heart-to-heart. I keep forgetting how impressionable you are… D'you ever fantasize what life would have been like had you been born white?

MARVIN: … No.

SAM: Rich instead of poor.

MARVIN: Not really.

SAM: Well, not even rich. Middle class. Comfortable. Life planned out for you the moment you come screaming into the world. Nice home, good clothes, never a rumble of hunger… decent schools…university – matter of course… then… one of the professions. Made for life. Everything smoothly plotted like a bestselling novel. Be lovely that wouldn't it? Admit it. Aces. Instead…instead, Marvin, you got dealt the worst possible hand: a poor, ignorant, Scouse nigger. (*Little pause.*) I know. It's a terrible word. Scouse. Lowest of the low. (*Little pause.*) Ignorant – not unintelligent; poor – no question. And nigger – most definitely. No hiding from that.

MARVIN: … Are you going anywhere with this?

SAM takes out his wallet, pulls out an old photograph, hands it to MARVIN.

SAM: Little Sam MacDonald. Seven years old. Raggedy-arsed little Toxteth scamp. Not far from where you used to live actually. Lily MacDonald. My mum. As white as Mother Teresa's conscience. And Benjamin MacDonald. My dad. Black as the ace of spades.

Pause.

MARVIN: Your dad was black?

SAM: And a lazy, feckless drunk… Terrific singer though.

Pause.

MARVIN: Am I meant to be…moved or something?

Pause.

SAM: Life's a genetic lottery Marvin. And I'm not ignorant of the fact that the black race has many fine and beautiful qualities. But was I glad the good Lord saw fit to colour me white? You can bet your black arse I was. One less obstacle in my path. One less mountain to climb.

MARVIN: Well, lucky you.

Pause.

SAM: There's only one colour that really matters, Marvin. The colour of money. Forget all the other bullshit.

MARVIN: And it doesn't matter how you get it.

SAM: There's no such thing as clean wealth. Stop deluding yourself. The leader of the 'free world' would fuck his own grandmother up the arse for a barrel of oil. (*Pause.*) Take or get took, Marvin. The game of life. Here endeth the lesson. (*Knocks back his drink.*) Right, I've got a job for you. That moaning little faggot on Ullet Road. Sort him out will you.

MARVIN: What d'you mean?

SAM: Put the frighteners on him. Better not do it yourself. Here… (*Hands over some bank notes.*)… slip someone a few bob.

MARVIN: What's he done?

SAM: Rubbed me up the wrong way. Only threatened me with the Environmental Health. Fucking upstart. Had him on the phone this afternoon, screeching his little head off about rats… I can't stand queers. They give me the creeps. Bunch of kiddie fiddlers, the lot of them.

Pause.

MARVIN: Why don't you just send someone in to deal with the rats? It'd be cheaper wouldn't it? In the long run. Instead of all this hassle.

SAM: Just do it Marvin. Do it tonight.

MARVIN: I can't. I've got something on.

SAM: Like what?

MARVIN: I'm taking my mum out.

Pause. MARVIN rises to leave.

SAM: You know, Marvin, when I walked into that gym all those months ago, and I stood there, watching you lift those weights like they were made of balsa wood… watching you beat the shit out that punch bag…sizing you up in the changing room… The *Guardian* sticking out your bag… I thought, hello, I've found myself a little gem here. Not your usual…mouth-breathing…knuckle-trailing…lobotomy case. No. This lad'll go places. He'll make a name for himself. And I can help him. I can nurture him, shape his destiny, educate him in the ways of the world. (*Little pause.*) But no, deep down, he's just a mummy's boy with scruples…who wants to be a fucking accountant for chrissake!

Little pause.

MARVIN: Businessman.

SAM: And what business would that be? Exactly.

Little pause. MARVIN exits.

Scene Seventeen

CLIFF's House. Kitchen.

CHERYL and JIMMY at the table. Meal finished. Two empty bottles of wine on the table. CHERYL is clutching the third bottle – as well as her glass. She's very drunk. JIMMY's quietly amused throughout.

CHERYL: … but we're *meant* to be a talkative people, aren't we? Us Irish. We are. It's in our genes or something. We're famed for it. The world over. Yakety-yak. We love the craic. Ah, we do, we do, we do. Go on, go on, go on. Would yer just listen to us talk our lives away. Why, we live for the craic. It's better than food. Sit down love, join in the craic. Hello there, fella, join the group why don't yer? Tell us yer life story. (*Drinks.*) And where I come from, how yer talk is who yer are… 'Ah, Brendan Flaherty, now he's a lovely fella, what a way with words he has.' And it's all bollocks, 'cause Brendan Flaherty's a lying, cheating little gobshite. He is. And would yer just listen to him playing up the lilt whenever there's an English girl nearby. Like some feckin' eejit in some stupid Hollywood film. I swear to Jesus he said 'top o' the mornin'' once. (*Drinks.*) He likes the English girls does Brendan Flaherty. And d'yer want to know why? Shall I'll tell yer why? I'll tell yer why. But keep this under yer hat. Yer might not know this, but English girls are sluts. That's right. Out and out sluts. All of them. Just mad for the sex they are. This is what Brendan thinks 'cause this is the pearl of wisdom passed down to Brendan by his great feckin' red-nosed loon of a Da. English girls are sluts and Irish girls are all… apprentice nuns.

She drinks, tops up her glass.

This is exceptionally good wine… Isn't it?… Isn't it?… Isn't it though? Where was I?… Oh yeah, talking. I was never one for the talking. I don't trust talky people with their gobs running away with them and their brains always struggling to catch up…this endless torrent of meaningless words…this…this…this…this…this relentless stream of utter *shite*…and I come to Liverpool and I'm thinking, great, a change from Dublin… and *it's worse!* They *never* shut up. It's like…it's like they're so desperate to *be* Irish they're trying to outdo us or something. And everyone, I'm telling yer, *every*one in this city is a feckin' comedian. This fella, this fella down at the college, he took to calling me Marcel…because I was so quiet. Yer know, Marcel Marceau. Oh, how he laughed at that one. (*Scouse accent:*) 'All right, Marcel. How's it goin' Marcel? Been stuck in any glass boxes lately, Marcel?' Prick.

She drinks, tops up her glass.

Where was I?… Oh yeah, the talking. I've no time for it. And d'yer want to know why I've no time for it? Shall I tell yer why? I'll tell yer why. (*Pause.*) 'Cause it's corrupt. (*Pause.*) Language. It's rotten. It is. It's the natural medium of the liar. Words were invented to hide things. Not explain them. (*Drinks.*) I can't abide liars. Shape-shifting bastards. I'd like to take every liar in the whole wide world, every last one of them, and tie them all together by their rotten, thieving tongues…and…and…and thieves is what they are… stealing yer love…stealing yer life…picking the pockets of yer soul…just robbing yer of…every…last…… selfish fuckers. (*Pause. She helps herself to some more wine… only the bottle's empty.*) Ah now…that's a sight to bring a tear to yer eye.

Pause.

JIMMY: This Brendan fella… he really hurt you.

CHERYL: … What?!… *Brendan?*… Brendan *Flaherty?* I'm not talking about that longwinded, spotty little gobshite. (*Long pause.*) I was talkin' about me Ma. (*Pause.*) Me gran used to say that some women are just a bruise waiting to happen… Emotionally. Yer know what I mean? (*Pause.*) She never had much luck with… (ah fuck it.)

Long pause.

JIMMY: Cliff told me your mum…

CHERYL: Died. Yeah. C'est la vie. (*Long pause.*) I wonder what's keeping him.

JIMMY: He's probably got a run in his nylons.

CHERYL: Yeah… He's a funny little fella. (*Pause.*) I thought he was a nosey old hen at first…but he's sweet, isn't he? Isn't he though? That rare thing…a decent human being. They should stick him in a museum or something. (*Long pause.*) So, Mister Quiet Man…what brought you to Liverpool? (*Pause.*) So much for the chirpy cockney.

JIMMY: I followed a girl up here… Woman.

CHERYL: … Is that it? That's not much of a story there fella. There'd be no free Guinness for you where I come from.

JIMMY: There's not much to tell. It…didn't work out.

CHERYL: Why?

JIMMY: She wasn't who I thought she was.

CHERYL: And who did yer think she was?

JIMMY: I forget.

Pause.

CHERYL: But yer stayed here anyway.

JIMMY: I like the place.

CHERYL: Yer *do?*

JIMMY: Yeah. The people are straight with you. Most of them.

Long pause. CHERYL looks at JIMMY's face closely.

…What?

CHERYL: I just noticed… haven't yer got lovely long eyelashes?

Pause.

CLIFF: (*Off.*) Almost ready.

CHERYL tries to make a whistling sound by running her wet finger round the rim of the glass…

JIMMY: So…how's this…gap year working out for you?

CHERYL: (*Bristly.*)… It's working out just grand. Thanks for asking.

Pause.

JIMMY: You know, it's none of my business…

CHERYL: That's right.

Little pause.

JIMMY: I just thought –

CHERYL: What? Yer'd be playing the good Samaritan?

JIMMY: Not exactly.

CHERYL: Yer'd be coming round here to dish out a little charity. Trying to make yerself feel better? Is that it?

JIMMY: No.

CHERYL: So what is it then? What are yer after?

JIMMY: I'm not after anything.

CHERYL: Don't lie. Everyone's after something. I might be drunk but I'm not stupid.

JIMMY: No one said you were stupid.

CHERYL: Good. Otherwise I'd be asking yer to step outside… What are yer laughing at? I could take yer in a fight and no mistake. I might be small but I'm wary.

JIMMY: Wiry.

CHERYL: Yeah! So watch it… You…just…watch it.

She points a threatening finger at him…then, suddenly, she passes out, her head resting on the table, but still holding the bottle and glass. JIMMY takes the bottle and glass from her, puts them on the table. Off stage, CLIFF makes the noise of a drum roll. Then hums the bass intro to 'Wilkommen' from Cabaret.

CLIFF: (*Off, singing.*) 'Wilkommen, Bienvenue, Welcome, Fremde, Etranger, Stranger.'

A stockinged-leg appears…

CLIFF: (*Off, singing.*) 'Glücklich zu sehen, Je suis enchanté, Happy to see you, Bliebe, Reste, Stay.
Wilkommen, Bienvenue, Welcome,
Im Cabaret, Au Cabaret, To Cabaret!'

CLIFF enters, in drag, sans make-up. He, too, is very drunk.

'Mein Damen und Herren, mesdames et monsieurs, comment ça va? Do you feel good? I am your host! Leave your troubles outside! So…life is disappointing? Forget it! In here life, is beautiful! The girls…are…beauti -…' What's up with Cheryl?

JIMMY: She talked herself into a coma.

CLIFF: But I haven't done my Vivien Leigh yet. Balls!… I was gonna do the scene where they take her away at the end of the movie. 'Whoever you are – I have always depended on the kindness of strangers.' (*Pause.*) What d'you let her drink so much for? (*Pause.*) Ah…look at her… look…she's kind of cute isn't she? (*Pause.*) Don't you think she's cute?

Pause.

JIMMY: Well, it's time I was going. Thanks for the meal.

CLIFF: Hang on, hang on, you can't just leave her there.

JIMMY: What d'you want me to do?

CLIFF: Put her to bed.

JIMMY: Me?

CLIFF: Well, *I* can't carry her up the stairs can I? Not in this. I'll go arse over tit.

JIMMY lifts CHERYL up into his arms. She sleepily throws her arms around his neck.

JIMMY: Where to?

CLIFF: Top floor.

JIMMY: … Top floor?

CLIFF: Oh stop your moaning, it's only four flights.

The 'brick wall' descends. The hooded youth appears and sprays onto the wall: DONT LET THE PACKIES TAKE ARE JOBS!

Scene Eighteen

MACEY's Flat. Kitchen.

MOHAMMED is sat on a straight-backed chair, with his head tilted back, his face hidden from us. He's holding a bunch of sorry-looking flowers. Pause. He raises his head: he has a black eye, a cut lip and a bloodied nose. His 'Versace' shirt is covered in blood. He takes out a handkerchief and spits some blood into it. MACEY enters with a bowl of water and first aid box.

MACEY: I said keep yer head back. I don't want yer bleeding all over me floor.

MOHAMMED: I get…head is spinning what is word? Dozy?

MACEY: Dizzy.

MOHAMMED: And blood goes into throat.

MACEY: So gargle and swallow. Head back.

She begins tending to him…

How many of them were there?

MOHAMMED: Boys? Four. Big boys.

MACEY: I told yer not to come round here again. Didn't I? Yer silly bleeder.

Pause.

MOHAMMED: Boys say I take job from them.

MACEY: Pushing drugs now are yer?

MOHAMMED: Drug? I no understand.

MACEY: Never mind…

MOHAMMED: … Boys also walk on flower. Sorry.

He holds them out to her, she puts them on the table.

MACEY: Stop buying me flowers, Mo. Yer must have better things to spend your money on… They've done a fine job on yer eye.

MOHAMMED: Boys no do this to eye. I get this in house of ale. This man, he go crazy. He think I steal beer. Was little bit left. I think he finish.

MACEY: Keep yer bloody head back will you!…What were yer doing in an ale house?

MOHAMMED: I have job now, Macey. Is what I come to tell you. I work in house of ale. Soon you no have to work in factory. You have more time with children. Is right place for mother.

She puts some iodine on a cut. He screams.

What you do?!

MACEY: Iodine.

MOHAMMED: It hurt.

MACEY: It's meant to hurt. It's good for yer.

MOHAMMED: Pain is good for you?

MACEY: Sometimes. Come here. (*She puts a plaster on his cut.*) There.

MOHAMMED: Thank you Macey.

She packs away the first aid box.

MACEY: Stop looking at me like that.

MOHAMMED: I cannot help. (*Pause.*) 'Underground, overground, wombling free…'

Beat. MACEY smiles. MOHAMMED smiles.

MACEY: You're off yer head.

MOHAMMED: And off my cak-k-ke also. (*Pause.*) I have surprise for you, Macey. In my pocket.

MACEY: Where have I heard that before?

MOHAMMED takes something from his trouser pocket, hands it to MACEY.

What's this?

MOHAMMED: Is ring.

MACEY: Yeah, I can see it's a ring.

MOHAMMED: Is ring for wedding. (*Little pause.*) Was ring of mother. (*Little pause.*) I save. All these years. To give to wife. (*Little pause.*) Is your ring now, Macey.

MACEY: I can't take this.

MOHAMMED: But it belong to you.

MACEY: No. I can't.

MOHAMMED: You no like?

MACEY: It's not a question of liking. Here. Just give it me on the day.

MOHAMMED: Please. Keep. It make Mohammed happy. It make Mohammed…word is pride?

MACEY: It's bad luck for the bride to have the ring before the wedding.

MOHAMMED: … Is true?… Well, we no want bad luck.

He puts the ring back in his pocket. Pause.

MACEY: Come on, yer'd better go.

MOHAMMED: I come again?

MACEY: No. And I mean it. It's not safe round here.

MOHAMMED: If boys beat Mohammed I can come again? Is worth beating to see your face.

MACEY: Listen Mo, I don't know how to say this without hurting yer feelings… (*Her business MOBILE begins to ring. She answers it…*) Hello?… No… No, I can't work tonight. I can't. Because. Because I'm busy. Suit yourself.

MOHAMMED: …Who was?

MACEY: Nobody.

MOHAMMED: Somebody. (*Little pause.*) Was factory? (*Little pause.*) They want you work every night? (*Little pause.*) Is not fair I think.

MACEY: All right, Mohammed. On yer way.

MOHAMMED: You should join union.

MACEY: Go on. I've got me cleaning to be getting on with.

MOHAMMED takes some money from his pocket.

MOHAMMED: Here Macey. Is wage. Is for you.

MACEY: (Jesus.) I can't...take...

MOHAMMED: No. Is OK. Is fine. You buy thing for children. Yes? Yes?

She knows it's futile to argue with him so she takes the money.

MACEY: OK. Right. Now see yerself out... Yer can go now, Mohammed.

MOHAMMED: OK. (*He leans forward for a kiss.*)

MACEY: ... What are yer doing?

MOHAMMED: Kiss.

MACEY: I don't do kissing... Just *go* will yer?

Little pause. MOHAMMED leaves. MACEY looks at the cash. She puts it in the ceramic jar.

The 'brick wall' descends. Two hooded youths: one is fly posting for the British Patriotic Front, putting posters over the Liverpool and Everton slogans. The other youth sprays the following: BATIL FOR BRITIN / WAR ON ASSYLIM / JOIN THE BPF.

Scene Nineteen

A neon sign is illuminated: HOTEL IMPERIAL. Amplified sound of a washing machine on its spin cycle. Lights up on:

Laundry Room.

SAMIR and BEHROUZ – dressed in hotel uniforms – are folding and stacking a great many bed sheets, ready for ironing. STELLA is sat away from them, engrossed in an article in the Sun *newspaper – occasionally she lets out a little grunt of disgust or displeasure. She's wearing a short denim skirt and a low cut top. (NB During this scene SAMIR and BEHROUZ occasionally speak in perfect RP English to reflect that they are speaking in their native tongue of Farsi.)*

BEHROUZ: (*RP.*)… Stella told me a wonderful piece of mythology about those birds…the Liver Birds?… Down by the waterfront?… Local tradition has it that they are, in fact, different sexes: the female bird, she faces the river, awaiting the sailors coming off the ships… while the male bird, he faces inland to see if the pubs are open.

SAMIR: Sluts and drunkards. How charming.

BEHROUZ: It's a joke, Samir!… Where's your sense of humour?

SAMIR: I left it back home. It doesn't travel well. (*Pause.*) You shouldn't have brought her in here…

BEHROUZ: She's not doing any harm… We're going into town.

SAMIR: You'll get in trouble.

BEHROUZ: What? Lose this lucrative job?

STELLA: Hey, Behrouz…

BEHROUZ: This isn't the only hotel in the city.

STELLA: Behrouz…how come yer never take me out in yer car?

BEHROUZ: … *Car?* What you talk, Stella?

STELLA: Well, it says here, yer all got special handouts for cars. Where's *yours?*

BEHROUZ: It was stolen, I think… You know what you Scousers are like.

STELLA pulls a disgusted face.

It was joke, Stella!… I take piss… Where your sense of humour?!

STELLA: I don't know, maybe someone nicked it.

BEHROUZ: (*Laughs.*) You are quick girl. Very quick girl. (*To Samir, RP.*) She has a wonderful sense of humour.

SAMIR: Yes. And whenever something is amusing, search it for a hidden truth.

BEHROUZ: … Meaning?

SAMIR: There's no smoke without fire, Behrouz. (*The sheet:*) This needs another clean!

He throws it to one side, gets another…

BEHROUZ: You don't like *any*thing about this city do you? Not a single thing. You're always complaining about the weather, the food, the pubs, the people.

SAMIR: I didn't ask to come to Liverpool.

BEHROUZ: None of us *asked* to come here.

SAMIR: Fold it properly, Behrouz.

BEHROUZ: Personally speaking, it's worked out just fine for me. I love the place.

SAMIR: You would.

BEHROUZ: What's *that* supposed to mean?

SAMIR: (*Another sheet:*) *This* too! For heaven's sake! I'm sick and tired of telling them about this!

He throws it to one side, gets another…

BEHROUZ: Tell me, Samir, exactly what were you hoping for? Really? When you came to this country?

SAMIR: Why won't they ever buy us some decent detergent?!

BEHROUZ: Little village in the country? Babbling brook? Spot of croquet after lunch?

SAMIR: How are we meant to do our job properly when they insist on buying the cheapest sodding… ?!

BEHROUZ: *You're* not sleeping on them, what does it matter?

SAMIR: I'm old fashioned, I take pride in my work.

BEHROUZ: And I thought this work was beneath you.

SAMIR: It *is* beneath me. (*Pause.*) I was the mayor of my city. The *mayor.* Elected. Twice. (*Pause.*) I've got two degrees. I ran my own business. I employed two hundred people. (*Pause.*) My family…for generations… (*Pause.*) Back home I was… But here…?

BEHROUZ: Here you're equal. (*Pause.*) No special privileges.

SAMIR: It's not a question of privilege.

BEHROUZ: … No?

Little pause. SAMIR's mobile rings. He exits to take the call in private.

STELLA: What's got *his* knickers in a twist?

BEHROUZ: Knickers? He no wear knickers.

STELLA: No. But he's got a right cob on, hasn't he?… He's in a *bad mood.*

BEHROUZ: Yes. You are right. Samir is not happy bunny today.

STELLA: Why?

BEHROUZ: His life is not what he wish for.

STELLA: He wants to join the queue.

BEHROUZ: … What queue?

STELLA: Never mind.

BEHROUZ: Hey Stella, what we do today?

STELLA: Well, I thought we could go into town, get something to eat, have a few drinks.

BEHROUZ: Get 'shit-faced?'

STELLA: No. Soft lad. Just a few drinks. Then go and see a movie.

SAMIR returns. He and BEHROUZ continue folding sheets…

SAMIR: (*RP.*) That was Mohammed…

BEHROUZ: Is he still traipsing through the Dingle? Searching for The Wombles?

SAMIR: … Mbusso lost his application.

BEHROUZ: (*Stunned.*) No?! They're not…?… *Mbusso?* They're not letting *Mbusso* in?!… But… That can't be right… I don't believe it.

SAMIR: Believe it.

Long pause.

BEHROUZ: How is he? Mbusso?

SAMIR: How do you think? He's devastated. (*Long pause.*) And what about *you*, Behrouz? Hmm? What will you do when your application is refused?

BEHROUZ: '*When?*'

SAMIR: A blind man could see through your lies.

Pause.

BEHROUZ: If they turn me down… I'll go underground. Hide out.

SAMIR: Live like a criminal.

BEHROUZ: If I have to.

SAMIR: Your parents will be so proud.

BEHROUZ: At least they'll be getting some money. I'll always find work here. (*Little pause.*) I know one thing, I won't hang around like Shpetim, waiting to be picked up. If and when that letter arrives, you won't see me for dust.

SAMIR: Living rough. Sleeping with one eye open. Dreading every knock on the door. What kind of life is that?

BEHROUZ: Better than the one I had back home, Samir. Better than that.

Pause.

SAMIR: People like you…you make it difficult for everyone else.

BEHROUZ: 'People like me?'

SAMIR: One person lies, they think we *all* lie.

BEHROUZ: Oh, you'd rather I'd been tortured? (*Pause.*)
You'd rather Shpetim had been tortured? (*Pause.*) I'm sorry
I've got no scars, Samir. No wounds. No…badge of honour.
I'm just a poor farm boy who wants a better life. That's my
crime. String me up. (*Pause.*) Anyway, if all else fails, I'll
marry an English girl.

SAMIR: You couldn't afford it.

BEHROUZ: Not like Mohammed. Properly. Someone I love.

SAMIR: … Oh. I see. (*Little pause.*) I suppose if she gave
herself so quickly it *must* be love. (*Little pause.*) Love grows
in the strangest places in this country…in doorways and
alley ways…amongst the rubbish and weeds…the air thick
with the aroma of vomit and urine.

BEHROUZ: Careful Samir, I have feelings for the girl.

SAMIR: Because she spreads her legs for you?

BEHROUZ: More than that.

SAMIR: Pleasures you with her mouth?

BEHROUZ stops folding sheets, glares at SAMIR. Pause.

BEHROUZ: I am finished for today.

SAMIR: Ten more minutes, Behrouz.

BEHROUZ: I am finished for today. (*To STELLA.*) I go get
change. Back in jiffy.

BEHROUZ exits. SAMIR continues working on the sheets…

STELLA: D'yer wanna a hand with that?

SAMIR ignores her.

Bit difficult on yer own.

SAMIR ignores her.

Yer don't like me very much, do yer Samir?… I can see it
in yer eyes.

SAMIR: I do not know you.

STELLA: No, yer don't. But yer've got me marked down as some sort of slapper, haven't yer? I can tell.

SAMIR: Slapper?

STELLA: Tart. Scrubber. Slag… Easy.

Pause.

SAMIR: You like Behrouz, Stella?

STELLA: Yeah.

SAMIR: You have feelings for him?

STELLA: Yeah, I do.

SAMIR: Why?

STELLA: Why? Because he's…different. Because he's not like all the other divvies round here. (*Pause.*) I also happen to think he's 'fit as fuck'.

SAMIR: You sleep with every boy you like?

STELLA: Would yer believe me if I said no?

Pause.

SAMIR: I do not understand girls in this city. Young women. At night, they drink too much. They raise skirt. They lower top. They…make toilet in the street. They have no self-respect.

Pause.

STELLA: I don't understand asylum seekers. I mean, they're all scroungers, aren't they? They all want somethin' for nothin'. They're all tryin' to steal our jobs. They're all dirty. They're all stupid. They've all got diseases… And yer know what? I bet most of them are terrorists… I wouldn't trust them as far as I could throw them.

Pause. BEHROUZ enters in his casual clothes.

BEHROUZ: I am ready… We go now, Stella… Come. We go.

STELLA: (*The* Sun.) Yer wanna be careful who yer listen to, Samir. (*To BEHROUZ.*) And you! If yer ever buy this shite again I'll ram it up yer hole!

BEHROUZ and STELLA exit. SAMIR continues folding sheets. Lights down to black.

Scene Twenty

CLIFF's bed sit. Night.

MARVIN in bed, CLIFF sitting on the edge of the bed. Remains of a take away pizza in its carton on the bed. (MARVIN still has the plaster on his face.)

CLIFF: … and she looks up at the sky and then she says to Mitch… (*Blanche DuBois:*) … 'There's so much – so much confusion in the world. Thank you for being so kind! I need kindness now.' (*Pause. Himself:*) And lights slowly down… OK. Scene Four. The following morning…

MARVIN sneaks a look at his watch…

Stella's lying down in the bedroom. And she's got this sort of…glazed look on her face…that look I get sometimes… and you just know that Stanley's been fucking her senseless the whole night. Well, that's his solution to everything. He's probably had her every which way. And Stella, well, she's just a martyr to her fanny as far as Stanley's concerned…she can't help herself. So, she's lying there, Stella, all dreamy-eyed, post-coital bliss etched onto her face, and Blanche enters, and she looks like shit, hasn't slept the whole night…

MARVIN can't stop himself from yawning…

MARVIN: It's been a long day. Sorry.

CLIFF: No. I broke my own rule. Always leave them wanting more. (*He kisses MARVIN – a long, slow, affectionate kiss.*) We'll do scene four next time. (*Eats a little pizza.*) You know, I had a sudden *déjà vu* moment the other day…this is all very *Kiss of the Spiderwoman.*

MARVIN doesn't get the reference.

Oh, I've got so much to teach you.

CLIFF gets under the sheets. Simultaneously, MARVIN gets out of bed and begins getting dressed. Pause.

Why don't you stay the night? (*Pause.*) Well, just stay a little longer then. (*Pause.*) I could open a bottle of wine. I've got a nice Rioja. (*Pause.*) We could watch a video.

MARVIN: I can't.

CLIFF: Something *you* want to watch. Claude Van Damme or something. I don't mind.

MARVIN: It's late.

CLIFF: I'm sure your mother can survive for one night without you. (*Pause.*) From what you've told me, your mother's tough as old boots. (*Pause.*) I don't suppose you've told her yet.

MARVIN: Told her what?

Pause.

CLIFF: You haven't got the bottle.

MARVIN: It's got nothing to do with bottle.

CLIFF: So tell her.

MARVIN: No.

CLIFF: Why?... Why?

MARVIN: I don't stick my nose into *her* sex life, I don't see why she has to know about mine.

CLIFF: Well, it's not *just* about sex, is it?

MARVIN: Oh. No. I forgot. With you people it's a whole way of life.

CLIFF: 'You people'?

MARVIN: Look. Just get off my case about this. OK? I'm not interested in joining your tribe.

105

CLIFF: Oh. And what tribe would that be? Precisely. (*Hits him with a pillow.*) Cheeky bastard.

Pause.

MARVIN: What does it matter, Cliff? Really?

CLIFF: Believe me, baby, it matters.

MARVIN: You're 'out' enough for both of us.

CLIFF: Don't make a joke out of this.

MARVIN: I'm not. But it's true. You're a one-man gay parade. With pink fireworks. And show tunes. Skipping along your yellow-brick road. (*Little pause.*) You don't half lay it on. (*Little pause.*) And as for all that drag crap. I'm sorry, but I think that's just…

CLIFF: I'm finished with drag.

MARVIN: Yeah? Really? So throw out the costumes.

CLIFF: … They're keepsakes. Mementos.

MARVIN: Masks more like. (*Pause.*) You hide behind your mask, Cliff, and let me hide behind mine.

CLIFF: But, the difference, Marvin, the crucial difference sweetheart…no one's under the slightest illusion that I'm straight. (*Pause.*) Look…look at me, Marvin… I know how hard it is. I do. I understand what you're going through.

MARVIN: No you don't. You're not me.

Little pause.

CLIFF: D'you really want to spend the rest of your life hiding in rooms? Skulking in dark corners? Sneaking off to other cities for sordid little…trysts…incognito?

Little pause.

MARVIN: You know the circles I move in… I've got an image to maintain.

CLIFF: Oh well. We don't want to mess with your image now, do we? God forbid.

Little pause.

MARVIN: I'm not your little gay project. OK? So stop trying to change me. I mean it, Cliff. 'Cause it's really starting to get on my tits. (*The plaster, bandage:*) I got *this* because I listened to you. ('Try and see the good in people.') Christ.

CLIFF: So…you don't mind me blowing you a couple of times a week just as long as no one knows about it.

MARVIN: Yeah, that's about the size of it. Get over it.

Pause.

CLIFF: No. This isn't you. You're not cold. One thing I pride myself on, Marvin… I have good intuition about people. And I wouldn't feel anything for you if I thought you were this callous. (*Pause.*) I'm not trying to change you, you daft sod. I just want you to be yourself. I want you to…fulfil your potential. You're more than a pair of fists. (*Pause.*) OK. All right. Let's strip this down to something basic shall we? Let me ask you this: do you love me? (*Pause.*) Questions don't come much simpler, Marvin.

Sound of the violin from CHERYL's room above. CLIFF and MARVIN both look up. It's beautiful. They listen…

MARVIN: She hasn't got much time.

CLIFF: I'm doing what I can. (*Pause.*) Isn't there something *you* could do?

MARVIN: Like what?

CLIFF: Talk him out of it.

Stupid suggestion. Pause. CLIFF hands him a notepad and pen.

Here.

MARVIN: … What?

CLIFF: I want you to write down ten things you like about me. Go on. I'm curious.

MARVIN: Oh behave.

CLIFF: Indulge me. Ten things. Starting with 'fine fellatrix'. Sorry – 'fella*tor*'.

MARVIN: I haven't got time for this.

CLIFF: Make time. (*Pause.*) *Five* things then.

MARVIN: Look. I have a really good time when I come here. *Here.* Just you and me. I'm not interested in 'out there'.

CLIFF: This room, it's just another bloody closet to you, isn't it?

MARVIN: It's about the size of one.

Little pause.

CLIFF: You don't take me seriously.

MARVIN: I thought this was meant to be fun.

CLIFF: It is. But I won't be treated like your bit on the side… your dirty little secret. I just won't.

MARVIN: I don't know what else you want from me, Cliff.

CLIFF: Well, believe it or not, stud, it's not just your great, fantastic body I'm interested in… How about a little commitment? Eh? How about a little intimacy? I'm getting too old for one night stands.

MARVIN: Oh come off it. This isn't a one night stand.

CLIFF: No. It's been twenty-three one night stands. Correction. Twenty-four. Look at me, I'm thirty years of age and, like it or not – and I don't – the bloom, ever so slightly, but ever so surely, is beginning to slip from the rose, darling. (*Little pause.*) I found a white hair on my balls yesterday.

MARVIN laughs.

It's not funny. (*Little pause.*) People age quickly in my family. And they die young. (*Little pause.*) I'm *really* too old to be the plaything of some sexually ambivalent closet case. (*Pause.*) The truest thing I ever heard? The heart is a lonely hunter. (*Pause.*) Kenny and John, I brought them together. Vikram and Steve. Jason and Dylan. That's what I do: I bring people together. But nobody ever brings *me* together.

Pause. MARVIN goes to kiss CLIFF, but CLIFF withdraws.

I don't feel we can carry on like this, Marvin. I mean it. If you can't commit then perhaps…well…maybe it's better we just ended things now.

Little pause.

MARVIN: Oh come on. (*Little pause.*) You're not serious?

Little pause.

CLIFF: Take me seriously, Marvin.

Pause. MARVIN exits. CLIFF looks up, in response to CHERYL's music. Sound of fireworks in the distance.

Scene Twenty-One

JIMMY's Bistro. Morning.

BEHROUZ is finishing a greasy full English breakfast. STELLA is eating a piece of toast. MOHAMMED has his ever-present bottle of water.

MOHAMMED: … Wack-k.

BEHROUZ: Wack-k-k-k.

MOHAMMED: Wack-k-k.

BEHROUZ: Take further Mohammed. Don't be shy. Wack-k-k-k.

MOHAMMED: Wack-k-k-k-k-k.

BEHROUZ: No. Too far. Now it sound like you have something stuck in throat.

STELLA: You're mental. Yer'll be growing a muzzy and getting your hair permed next.

BEHROUZ: What you mean?

STELLA: I mean yer a head case.

BEHROUZ: Off my cak-k-ke?

STELLA: Big time.

BEHROUZ: Well, you must be off your cak-k-ke also, to fall in love with crazy guy like me.

STELLA: Oh, 'love' now, is it?

Little pause. She dips her toast in his egg…

Don't half fancy yourself don't yer?

BEHROUZ: Fancy *you* more.

BEHROUZ and STELLA eat from opposite ends of the piece of toast and end up in a kiss.

OK Mohammed, try once more.

MOHAMMED: Wack-k-k-k.

BEHROUZ: Good.

MOHAMMED: Hello wack-k-k-k. All right wack-k-k-k.

BEHROUZ: Much better.

MOHAMMED: But this I say only to old men?

BEHROUZ: Right.

MOHAMMED: And to young men…?

BEHROUZ: Mate.

MOHAMMED: Hello mate.

BEHROUZ: Or La.

MOHAMMED: La?

BEHROUZ: All right, La. Good to see yer, La. How's it goin' La?

MOHAMMED: How is what going?

BEHROUZ: Life Mohammed. Life.

MOHAMMED: There is lot to keep in brain with this language. What is meaning of 'La'?

STELLA: It's short for lad.

MOHAMMED: Is just *one* letter short? So… *'gir'* will be short for girl? Hello gir. How's it goin', gir?

STELLA: (*Laughing.*) Er…no. It doesn't work like that… Don't worry, Mo, you'll pick it up. Just try not to lay it on 'thick-k-k-k-k-k', like this nutter. Right. I'm off.

BEHROUZ: Where you off?

STELLA: Work. Soft lad.

BEHROUZ: I see you later?

STELLA: Is the Pope a Catholic?

BEHROUZ: … Yes.

STELLA: Then you'll see me later.

STELLA kisses BEHROUZ then exits.

BEHROUZ: (Is Pope a Catholic?)

Pause.

MOHAMMED: Is good for you to give me lesson. Thank you, Behrouz.

BEHROUZ: No problem.

Pause.

MOHAMMED: At one time, I no think you like me. I understand. I walk with band and I get money. Is not fair I know. (*Pause.*) Is better now I have job. Is good for man to have proper job and bring home bacon.

BEHROUZ: … Bring home bacon?

MOHAMMED: Is expression… Bacon is money.

BEHROUZ: (*A joke.*) I no think Muslim should be bring home bacon.

Pause.

MOHAMMED: You happy person I think since you meet Stella. You get fat. Is sign of happy.

BEHROUZ looks at his belly. Pause.

You are lucky man, Behrouz. Stella…she is very nice girl. She bring light to your life.

BEHROUZ: Stella is Judy now.

MOHAMMED: … Her name is Judy?

BEHROUZ: No. Is just expression. It mean girlfriend.

MOHAMMED: Judy mean girlfriend?

BEHROUZ: And wife.

MOHAMMED: I feel I never learn this language. Is hard to learn *English* but this… (*Pause.*) I get extra lesson from Macey I think.

BEHROUZ: Oh, you get many lesson from Macey I think.

MOHAMMED: Yes. Many lesson.

BEHROUZ: She expert in lesson.

Pause.

MOHAMMED: Behrouz… I always get feeling you no like Macey. (*Pause.*) Is right this feeling?

Long pause.

BEHROUZ: You ever have girlfriend, Mohammed? Back home?

MOHAMMED: Yes. Once. But…was not to be.

Little pause.

BEHROUZ: She was pretty?

MOHAMMED: Was long time ago.

BEHROUZ: But, this girl, she have other thing you like, yes? As well as pretty. She was everything you would want in wife?

MOHAMMED: I no wish to talk, Behrouz. Past is over. I must look to future. Future is all.

Long pause.

BEHROUZ: Listen mate, I have thing to tell you. But I tell you as friend. Yes? I tell you as mate.

Pause.

MOHAMMED: What is thing to tell?

BEHROUZ: There is word in Liverpool…slapper.

Blackout. A BBC news report plays: a journalist reporting from Iraq, post-Saddam, describing a scene of devastation and carnage caused by insurgents. Over this, the sound of a small explosion…and another…and another. These are in fact… bangers.

Scene Twenty-Two

The House: Kitchen.

Lights up on CHERYL, sat at the table, head down, sipping tea. There is a big stack of note paper on the table and a pen. She flinches as another banger goes off. Pause. Then the off stage sounds of metal on concrete, metal on wood. Clearly, somebody is in frenzied pursuit of something. And it's not going smoothly whatever it is. Another banger goes off. CHERYL flinches again. From the cellar, exclamations in Kurdish. Sound of metal on something soft, squelchy. Exclamation of triumph from MOHAMMED…

Pause. MOHAMMED enters holding a thick metal bar in one hand, a cardboard box under his arm, and a huge dead rat in his other hand. He is wearing protective Wellington boots and rubber gloves, both of which are too big for him. He looks knackered. In addition to his black eye, he now has a plaster over the bridge of his nose.

MOHAMMED: Oh…hello Miss. Sorry for trouble. I no think people home. (*Beat.*) I think is last one. (*Pause.*) I sorry if I make big noise. Disturb you. (*Pause.*) This one mother I think. She make big fight. (*Counts the dead rats inside the box…*) What is four more than ten?

CHERYL: … Fourteen.

MOHAMMED: Fourteen. And *this?* Fiveteen?

CHERYL: *Fif*teen.

MOHAMMED: *Fif*…teen? (*He drops the dead rat into the box.*) Fifteen rat. (*He spits in the box.*) All dead. No more problem with rat. (*Pause.*) Is tea you drink?

CHERYL: Would yer like some?

MOHAMMED: If OK. I have big thirst… Please, no milk. Tea is fine. Is hard work to kill rat. And is difficult to see… Thank you. Very kind.

Silence. They drink.

CHERYL: What happened? Yer eye. Yer nose. The cut on yer face.

MOHAMMED is reluctant to explain. Pause.

MOHAMMED: This… (*His nose:*)… this is from fight with friend.

CHERYL: Yer friend?

MOHAMMED: Yes. He say big insult about wife so we fight. So we friend no more. (*Pause.*) This eye I get from man in ale house. He think I steal…no matter. Is sob story. Cut is from boys on street.

Pause.

CHERYL: People are horrible.

MOHAMMED: No. Is good and bad. Where you go is always good and bad. Is good people here. Many good people. Mister Cliff. Mister Jimmy. Mister Sam.

Silence.

CHERYL: Where are yer from?

MOHAMMED: Everton. Is other side of city.

CHERYL: I meant originally.

MOHAMMED: First, you mean? Kurdistan.

CHERYL: Yer a refugee? (*Pause.*) Do yer have family back home?

MOHAMMED: I have family in heart. Is only place.

Pause.

CHERYL: Do yer ever get homesick?

MOHAMMED: Sick for home?… Halabja was pretty town. But now? For me? Is town for ghost.

CHERYL: Yer from Halabja?

MOHAMMED: Is small town. Is place nobody know.

CHERYL: I know about Halabja.

Little pause.

MOHAMMED: You know what happen in Halabja? What Saddam do? How you know?

CHERYL: I read a lot.

MOHAMMED: You are first I meet.

Little pause.

CHERYL: And yer family…? *All* yer family…? (*Pause.*) Yer poor man. Yer poor, poor man.

Pause.

MOHAMMED: I try make new life. Is long way to come for new life. But is place for Mohammed. I have dream one night. England is place to be free. (*Pause.*) You want know journey of Mohammed? You would be interest? (*He takes out a crumpled pocket map.*) Here. Kurdistan. Halabja. First, I make small journey to Iran. From Iran, I go Turkey. From Turkey I have chance. Is here I pay man for travel in truck. We hide in truck. Twelve refugee. We go Macedonia… Yugoslavia… Hungary… Slovakia… Republic of Czech… Germany… Belgium, I think…and then on water. On sea. I know is safe – on boat – when I see cliff which are white. Is thing we know.

CHERYL: What are these marks for?

MOHAMMED: Here. Old man die… Majid. He have big problem with heart but he no have medicine… We bury him in forest. (*Little pause.*) Here. There is woman from Saudi. She have baby. But baby…little girl…she not alive when born. (*Pause.*) I make mark to remember. (*Pause.*) I keep map for special reason. You know why? One day I show map to children. They know journey of father. And they have proud. Pride. Big pride.

Pause.

CHERYL: I wish I had yer courage.

MOHAMMED: For what you wish courage?

CLIFF enters, reacts to the box of dead rats.

CLIFF: Have you finished? Is that the last of them?

MOHAMMED: I think is last. You no have trouble now, Mister Cliff.

CLIFF: Next time Mohammed, you ask him for some traps or something. Some poison.

MOHAMMED: Mister Sam give me firework. Scare shit out of rat. (*He picks up the box of dead rats.*) Thank you for tea, Miss. Very kind… You find courage when you need.

MOHAMMED exits.

CLIFF: How could you sit in here while all that was going on? (*Pause.*) You want to try a walk in the garden?

CHERYL: No. Yeah. No. Later. Maybe later. I want to finish me letter.

Pause.

CLIFF: You're writing to your mum? (*Little pause.*) D'you find that helps?

CHERYL: Raj Persaud recommended it.

CLIFF: Friend of yours, is he? (*Pause.*) You've written an awful lot.

CHERYL: There's an awful lot to tell her.

CLIFF: Do you tell her everything? (*Long pause.*) I'm sure she'd rather you were getting on with your life.

Pause. SAM and MARVIN enter. SAM is holding a large envelope.

SAM: What's this then? Tenant's Co-operative? You sure you've got a quorum here?

CHERYL's rather flustered by SAM's presence. She gathers her papers together, ready to leave.

I've got something for you. (*Takes a small envelope from his inside pocket, hands it to her.*) Here.

CHERYL exits. Little pause. Looks are exchanged between MARVIN and CLIFF. SAM sits, pours tea into the mug MOHAMMED was using, sips, reacts unfavourably.

SAM: Jesus, what's this, No Frills? (*Pause.*) I believe all the rats are gone.

CLIFF: All but one.

Beat. SAM laughs…

SAM: You know, I have to hand it to you…you've certainly got a lot of balls for a little nonce. Most people would be shitting in their pants with Marvin in the room.

CLIFF: I'm not scared of him.

SAM: Oh aye? (*Little pause.*) Fancy your chances do you? (*Little pause.*) What d'you think, Marvin? Reckon you could take him?

CLIFF: … Doesn't have much to say for himself, does he?

SAM: Strong and silent type.

CLIFF: The bigger they come the harder they fall.

SAM: Are you fucking mental or something?… Oy! Joke's over. Let's get down to business. I've sorted out the rat problem. There's a plumber… Are you listening to me?

There's a plumber coming in next week to look at the sink and the toilet.

CLIFF: What about the roof?

SAM: The roof'll have to wait a couple of weeks. I've got a cash flow problem.

CLIFF: And you'll have a bigger cash flow problem when we don't pay you our full rent.

Pause.

SAM: You vex me, nonce.

CLIFF: I think the word you're searching for is *nance*.

Pause.

SAM: All right. I don't normally do this, but I'm gonna make you a deal.

SAM pushes the envelope towards CLIFF.

CLIFF: What's this?

SAM: Well, hopefully this'll make you happy. And get you off my back.

CLIFF opens the envelope and pulls out some photographs… which, one by one, repulse him, almost to the point of vomiting.

CLIFF: What the – ?! What is this?! What…?! You sick fuck! (*Flings the photographs back at SAM.*) They're disgusting!!

SAM produces a large plastic envelope. Carefully - without touching the prints – he puts the photographs into the plastic envelope and seals it.

CLIFF: … What are you doing?

SAM: Just protecting the evidence.

CLIFF: Evidence?… What fucking evidence?

SAM: Proof that I've got a paedophile living under my roof. Fingerprinted proof. Do we understand each other? Nonce.

CLIFF: You sick bastard. You-you-you…vile, repellent, repulsive…

SAM: Oh, stop it. You'll have me tossing and turning all night. Rent. The end of the week. Plus arrears.

SAM exits. Pause.

MARVIN: I didn't know anything about this. Honestly. I swear to you.

SAM: (*Off.*) Marvin!

CLIFF: … Your lord and master's calling. (*Little pause.*) Run along Marvin.

MARVIN exits. Pause. CHERYL enters, dejected, holding a letter…she hands it to CLIFF, sinks into a chair.

… Eviction?

CHERYL: Non-payment of rent.

CLIFF: He can't evict you. He can't just…

CHERYL: He never signed my rent book. Not once.

CLIFF: We won't let him evict you. We'll go to the Citizen's Advice… *I'll* go to the Citizen's Advice.

Lights down to black.

Birdsong. Lights slowly up. Morning. The 'brick wall' descends. All the racist graffiti and BPF posters have now been covered by a beautiful mural. An African scene, vivid, colourful, and painted by MBUSSO. Tins of different coloured paint surround him. He's putting the finishing touches to the mural…stands back, drinks from a bottle of whisky, takes in the scene, admires his work.

Scene Twenty-Three

The Registry Office.

MACEY and MOHAMMED, JIMMY, CLIFF and the REGISTRAR.

MOHAMMED is holding a bunch of flowers. He's in a sombre mood. He's angrily picking the petals off the flowers and dropping them on the floor.

REGISTRAR: I do solemnly declare…

MACEY: I do solemnly declare…

REGISTRAR: That I know not of any lawful impediment…

MACEY: That I know not of any lawful impediment…

REGISTRAR: Why I, Millicent Edith Lewis…

MACEY: It's Macey… Macey.

REGISTRAR: I have to go with what's on the birth certificate.

MOHAMMED: Ha! Even name is lie.

MACEY: Oh shut yer hole.

REGISTRAR looks at MOHAMMED ripping the petals and throwing them on the floor.

JIMMY: (*Explaining.*) It's a Kurdish custom.

MOHAMMED: What *you* know about custom?! You know nothing about custom of Kurdish people!

REGISTRAR: Your latest groom seems…a little agitated, Mr Baker.

JIMMY: He's fine. Please go on.

REGISTRAR: Why I, Millicent Edith Lewis…

MACEY: Why I, Millicent Edith Lewis…

REGISTRAR: May not be joined in matrimony to Mo-

MACEY: May not be joined in matrimony to Mohammed Reza Ahmadi. Yeah yeah. Can we get this over with?

MOHAMMED: In my country…we have family and relative and friend, in big hall, with music and dance and food and drink. And money is give to bride and husband. Is big celebration. Is great joy. In honour of husband. In honour of wife.

MOHAMMED – having torn every petal from every flower – hands MACEY the bunch of stems. MACEY takes them, throws them to one side.

MACEY: Jimmy, get a grip will yer.

REGISTRAR: What exactly is going on here?

JIMMY: Wedding day jitters.

REGISTRAR: More than jitters I'd say.

MACEY: Can we just get on with it? I've got places to be.

MOHAMMED lets out a loud exclamation at this.

I've got to pick *me kids* up!

Little pause.

REGISTRAR: You have the rings?

Awkward pause, people look at each other…

MACEY: Well, *I* didn't bring one!

MOHAMMED: I have ring. Ring which is sacred. But is not for use today.

Little pause.

REGISTRAR: Right. No rings.

CLIFF: (*Takes off his ring.*) Here. You can use this. If you want.

MOHAMMED declines CLIFF's offer…

REGISTRAR: Mohammed. Please repeat after me. I – Mohammed Reza Ahmadi… (*Little pause.*) Mohammed?

MOHAMMED: … I – Mohammed Reza Ahmadi.

REGISTRAR: Do take thee – Millicent Edith Lewis – to be –

MOHAMMED: Do *not* take thee – Macey Lewis – to be my lawful wedded wife.

REGISTRAR: … *Do* take thee. Millicent Edith –

MOHAMMED: Do *not* take thee!

REGISTRAR: Do…surely.

MOHAMMED: Do *not*. Surely.

REGISTRAR: I'm beginning to lose my patience. Is there some sort of problem?

MOHAMMED: Yes.

JIMMY: No.

MOHAMMED: Yes is problem. Wife is slapper.

REGISTRAR: … Excuse me?

MOHAMMED: Wife is prostitute. So will *not* be wife.

MACEY: Suit yerself yer mad fucker. It's no skin off my nose either way.

Little pause. REGISTRAR looks at JIMMY.

JIMMY: Can you give us five minutes? I can sort this out.

REGISTRAR: I do have another party booked in right after you.

REGISTRAR leaves.

JIMMY: Mohammed, sit down a minute… Mohammed. Please… Macey?

They both sit.

JIMMY: Mohammed. Look.

MOHAMMED: Mohammed look. But Mohammed no see. No see truth. Everything is lie. Is big joke, yes? People in Liverpool like big joke. Famous for big joke.

JIMMY: This is just business. Remember?

MOHAMMED: Business for you. Business for she. But for Mohammed, is not business.

JIMMY: Mohammed.

MOHAMMED: No. Is not business.

MACEY: Oh, what's the use? He's a head case.

MOHAMMED: I have pain, Macey. Pain in heart.

MACEY: Yer a pain in the *arse*.

JIMMY: Macey.

MOHAMMED: I have pain you no understand. I have pain come from love.

CLIFF: Well, that's the worst kind and no mistake.

Little pause.

MOHAMMED: You no see pain of Mohammed. My friend Samir, he say you no see any pain we have. He is true. Pain of asylum seeker no exist for we not people. We not human being. Is right.

MACEY: Yer can't be in love with me yer daft pillock. Yer don't even know me.

MOHAMMED: I *see* you I *know* you! I know you are woman for Mohammed.

CLIFF: Love at first sight.

MOHAMMED: Is right. What Mister Cliff say. *First* sight. My eye tell my heart. And now my heart in pain.

MACEY: It's all in yer head yer soft get.

MOHAMMED: Is not in head. I know difference and this pain is worse! DON'T TREAT ME LIKE NON-PERSON!

JIMMY: Mohammed, take it easy.

Pause.

MACEY: This is a waste of time. I came here to do yer a favour.

She rises to leave.

MOHAMMED: I *show* you! I *show* you how pain is worse!

MOHAMMED stands up and takes off his jacket…and then his shirt…revealing his torso completely disfigured with scars and wounds and burns. JIMMY, MACEY and CLIFF find it difficult to look.

Is worse than this. Is worse than beating. Is worse than stone. Is worse than stick. Is worse than cigarette. Is worse than bullet.

MOHAMMED breaks down in tears. Long pause. MACEY gently helps him on with his shirt, buttons it for him…

The REGISTRAR returns.

REGISTRAR: Well…? Do we have a wedding or not?

Pause.

CLIFF: I'll marry him if you won't.

End of Act Two.

ACT THREE

Scene Twenty-Four

Split Scene: Sefton Park / Cemetery. Morning.

Darkness. A Cappella African singing: 'Homeless' by Ladysmith Black Mambazo. Several bars of this before images become visible…first the 'moonlight sleeping on the midnight lake'…the colours slowly transform to reflect the reddy pink of the morning sky, bringing with it the dawn chorus of birdsong. And then…

Lights slowly up on MBUSSO dangling lifelessly from a tree. A stack of empty beer cans and liquor bottles scattered on the floor beneath him. Lights slowly down. An accordion accompanies the song…

Lights up on a freshly filled grave. SAMIR, MOHAMMED, BEHROUZ and STELLA are standing around the grave. SAMIR is playing his accordion. BEHROUZ is holding the ghetto blaster. The song ends. BEHROUZ turns off the ghetto blaster. Pause. SAMIR steps forward. Pause.

SAMIR: Inside this man…this man who was big with heart of lion… inside Mbusso Thomas Sibanda, there was spirit of child. (*Pause.*) In another life, this man…this man have glimpse of happiness…of what his God provide for happiness. He have pride in marriage, in family, in friendship. (*Pause.*) Mbusso Thomas Sibanda – like many who are here – like many who make this journey – Mbusso walk the rest of his days in shadow of death…death of wife…death of children…and heavy in heart of Mbusso… a truth he could not face…the lion was not strong enough to protect wife…to save children…to preserve life he feel his God want for him.

Pause. SAMIR nods to BEHROUZ who presses play on the ghetto blaster… this time something lively and uplifting in celebration of this man's life: 'The Rainmaker' by Hugh Masekela. Lights slowly down to black. Music segues into next scene, accompanied by the sound of thunder and rain…

Scene Twenty-Five

The Bistro. Afternoon.

MOHAMMED alone at a table, head bowed. CLIFF enters, mopping the floor. Music fades out…

CLIFF: … Sorry to hear about your friend.

> *Pause. JIMMY enters with a mug of coffee and a glass of water. He sits with MOHAMMED. Pause.*

JIMMY: You OK? (*Little pause.*) Can I get you anything else?

MOHAMMED: Water is fine. (*Pause.*) He was beautiful man, Mister Jimmy. Very beautiful… I have big love for Mbusso… I love Mbusso very much… I am not like Mister Cliff.

JIMMY: Nobody's like Cliff.

CLIFF: More's the pity.

MOHAMMED: One time…I see him smile… Mbusso… I pretend read book while he watch TV…he like cartoon you have… The Simpson?… something happen in cartoon and he smile…big big smile…was one of most beautiful thing I see. (*Pause.*) Just one time I see him smile.

> *Pause.*

JIMMY: We have to work on your story soon. For your hearing. We have a lot to do, Mohammed.

MOHAMMED: What is point Mister Jimmy? Marriage is fake. Marriage is bullshit.

CLIFF: Most relationships are bullshit. I don't know anyone who's got an honest relationship.

JIMMY: … Do you mind?

CLIFF: … Sorry.

> *CLIFF exits with bucket and mop.*

JIMMY: Ignore him.

MOHAMMED: But Mister Cliff is right. Man from Immigration, he will see, he will know…

JIMMY: Which is why…

MOHAMMED: … Macey and Mohammed, is all…shit.

JIMMY: Listen to me, Mohammed…this is why we have to get your story spot on. We need to rehearse, yeah? Get the two of you singing from the same hymn sheet… Telling the same story.

MOHAMMED: … I no want see Macey.

JIMMY: You have to.

MOHAMMED: It hurt when I see Macey.

Little pause.

JIMMY: (*His 'heart'.*) You've got to try and turn this off.

MOHAMMED: How? How to turn off? Is not possible. Is like… is like to be dead.

Pause.

JIMMY: Macey wants to help you, Mohammed. She really does. She wants to help you stay in the country.

MOHAMMED: Yes. That is her job. You pay her money so is job for her. (*Looks at watch.*) And now I have job also.

JIMMY: Mohammed, just wait a minute…sit down. Tomorrow afternoon. OK? Macey's flat. She'll be waiting.

Pause.

MOHAMMED: And will just be *me* in Macey flat? Or will Mohammed be in big line of men? (*Little pause.*) And perhaps you in line of men also? (*Little pause.*) Is how you know Macey? You and she…?

JIMMY: … No.

MOHAMMED: Then how you know? Where you meet?

JIMMY: I don't know. I can't remember… It's not important.

Pause.

MOHAMMED: Me think your pants soon be on fire.

Pause.

JIMMY: Mohammed, do you want to stay in this country? Then let us help you.

Pause.

MOHAMMED: I have work now.

JIMMY: This job… this guy you're working for… I've been hearing some things.

MOHAMMED: Mister Sam is good man.

JIMMY: … How would you like a job here?

MOHAMMED: Here? In bistro?

JIMMY: Yes. Waiting tables. A waiter.

MOHAMMED: … No. I understand. You see scar of Mohammed and now you feel… I am not sure of word. Thank you, no.

JIMMY: It's not charity Mohammed. I really need a waiter.

CLIFF enters with a mug of coffee and a library book. He sits down at another table, lights up a cigarette.

MOHAMMED: You have waiter.

JIMMY: I need another. You'd be helping me out. I pay minimum wage.

MOHAMMED: I get minimum wage with Mister Sam. One pound fifty is OK for Mohammed. And he first to give job. So…

JIMMY: *One* pound…? I pay four pound fifty.

MOHAMMED: Bullshit. For waiter?

JIMMY: Four pound fifty is minimum wage.

MOHAMMED: … Is no lie?

JIMMY: Cliff, how much do I pay you? An hour?

CLIFF: Not enough.

JIMMY: Cliff.

CLIFF: Four pound fifty.

Pause.

MOHAMMED: I think about it.

MOHAMMED exits. JIMMY looks over at CLIFF…

JIMMY: What's up with you lately?

CLIFF: Oh, the usual: life, love, bad hair day. (*Little pause.*) I don't suppose there's any chance of you subbing me? I feel like going out and getting rat-arsed.

Pause. JIMMY takes out some cash and gives it to CLIFF.

I said, rat-arsed.

JIMMY gives him some more cash. Pause. He looks at the book…

JIMMY: Tenancy Law?

CLIFF: Cheryl.

JIMMY: … How is she?

CLIFF: Why don't you call round and see for yourself?

JIMMY: What good's that going to do?

CLIFF: Well, here's a shocker: she actually likes you… Yeah, I know, it's weird isn't it?

Pause.

JIMMY: She *said* she likes me?

CLIFF: Yeah. She gave me a note. She wants to meet you behind the bike sheds after school. (*Pause.*) Actually, what she said…she thinks you're interesting. Which is the same thing.

JIMMY: How's that the same thing?

CLIFF: God, you know nothing about women do you? (*Long pause.*) Have you ever been in love, Jimmy? (*Little pause.*) Have you?

JIMMY: Yeah. Once. Long time ago. Got over it.

CLIFF: Still picking at the scab though, aren't you?

Pause. JIMMY exits. Lights down.

Scene Twenty-Six

CHERYL's bed sit. Afternoon.

SAM is packing CHERYL's clothes and possessions into her suitcase and some bin bags.

CHERYL: No!… Please!

SAM: Time's up, Cheryl. You've had your notice.

CHERYL: I've got nowhere to go.

SAM: Not my problem. I thought this was going to work out. It isn't. And at the end of the day, business is business.

CHERYL: I'll do anything! Anything yer want.

SAM: Too late, love.

CHERYL: Anything yer ask. Anything at all.

SAM: You had your chance.

CHERYL: I'll try harder.

SAM: What? Move a muscle?

CHERYL: I can be better. I can. I will. I will. I promise. Please.

Pause.

SAM: Kiss me… I said, kiss me.

Pause. She kisses him on the mouth…

Dry. Twenty-two and you're dry as a fucking bone. It's not natural.

He continues packing her stuff away.

CHERYL: Oh God oh God oh God oh God oh God.

SAM: Get a grip.

CHERYL: Yer can't send me out there! Yer can't!

SAM: I can. I am.

She falls on her knees in front of him, sobbing.

CHERYL: Please…please, Mr MacDonald… Sam… I'm begging yer… I'll try the other thing…what yer said…yer business clients…

SAM: They'd be asking for a refund. It was a stupid idea.

CHERYL: Don't do this.

SAM: Let go.

MARVIN enters, unseen by SAM.

CHERYL: Yer don't have to do this. We can work something out. We can. If yer've any decent human feelings inside of yer…

SAM: You've drawn on my charity long enough, Cheryl. It's not a bottomless pit. Let go.

As SAM begins tying one bin bag, CHERYL begins removing stuff from another.

Hey! What are you – ?! Don't fuck about. HEY!… Stop that. I said, STOP IT!

SAM physically restrains her, throws her onto the bed.

Don't try my patience, girl! I mean it. You're wasting my time. Now, enough's enough… Marvin. I told you to wait in the car… Now you're here, make yourself useful. Dump her stuff out on the street… Well, don't just stand there Marvin. I haven't got all bleeding day.

MARVIN picks up a suitcase and a bin bag, exits. Pause. SAM picks up her birthday card…opens it…

You know what really pisses me off about you young people? You're weak. You're mollycoddled. You don't know when you're well off. My mam died when I was twelve. I didn't sit around whingeing about it. Day of the funeral I still did my paper round! (*He throws the card into one of the bin bags.*) It's about time you faced up to reality, Cheryl. Mummy's gone. OK? Mummy's dead. It's time to get on with your life. Somewhere else. Come on.

MARVIN enters, still carrying the suitcase and bin bag. He drops them onto the floor.

What d'you want, Marvin?… I said, dump her stuff on the street.

MARVIN takes a wad of notes from his pocket, peels off some, hands them to SAM.

MARVIN: Here.

SAM: What's this?

MARVIN: Her rent. Six months. Now leave her alone.

SAM: You what?

MARVIN: Leave. The girl. Alone.

Pause.

SAM: What's going on? (*Pause.*) What is this? (*Pause.*) Marvin. Go and wait in the car. Now.

MARVIN doesn't move…

D'you really know what you're doing? (*Little pause.*) For *this?* (*Little pause.*) She's a fucking tramp. (*Pause.*) Have you two…? Behind my back? (*Pause.*) Marvin. (*Pause.*) After all I've done for you. After all…you're throwing it away…you're throwing it back in my face…over a piece of rubbish like this? (*Long pause.*) I'd keep a low profile if I were you, Marvin.

MARVIN: Is that a threat?

SAM: Take it any way you want.

SAM exits. Pause. MARVIN and CHERYL look at each other.

CHERYL: Why?

MARVIN: Why not?

Scene Twenty-Seven

MACEY's Flat. Kitchen. Afternoon.

JIMMY and MOHAMMED. JIMMY has a rucksack at his feet. On the floor, a cardboard box full of toys and children's books.

MOHAMMED: Yahoo Chat? What is Yahoo Chat?

JIMMY: It's a room.

MOHAMMED: Room?

JIMMY: On the internet.

MOHAMMED: Internet. Right. And we meet in this room?

JIMMY: Yes. It's where the two of you first met. You started chatting with each other… then you started e-mailing each other… exchanged photographs… and gradually –

MOHAMMED: How we give photograph?

JIMMY: Over the internet.

MOHAMMED: Is possible?

JIMMY: Through e-mail, yes.

MOHAMMED: E-mail. Right.

MOHAMMED looks off…

JIMMY: Do you have e-mail, Mohammed?… Mohammed?

MOHAMMED: Macey is very worry about child.

JIMMY: Do you have e-mail?… No? OK. I'll nip down to the library and set you up with an e-mail address. (*Takes some sheets of paper from his rucksack.*) We can't fake any e-mails but we can try something with photographs. Here… I've scanned and downloaded some photographs of Macey.

MOHAMMED: She take good photograph. Camera like her face.

JIMMY: OK. Scrunch them up.

MOHAMMED: Please?

JIMMY: You have to make the photographs look old, battered, scrunched…here. (*Takes the photographs back, scrunches them up.*) You've carried these photographs with you all across Europe.

MOHAMMED: Ah.

MOHAMMED takes the photographs and scrunches and creases them.

JIMMY: And I'll need a couple of photographs of you… Do you have any photographs?

MACEY enters…

MOHAMMED: Little girl. She is OK?

MACEY: She's sleeping.

JIMMY: Mohammed, do you have any photographs of yourself?

MOHAMMED shakes his head 'no'. JIMMY takes a Polaroid instamatic from his rucksack.

OK. We'll do it here. Over there. Not by the window. By the wall, that's it.

MOHAMMED goes and stands by the wall. JIMMY prepares to take his photograph.

Smile Mohammed. You're sending this photo to the woman you love. Remember? Big smile. You want her to be impressed with your good looks.

MOHAMMED: She no think I'm handsome.

JIMMY: … Smile. (*Takes a photo…*) Stay there. One more for good luck. (*Takes another photo.*) OK. I'm going to nip down to the library. You carry on rehearsing until I get back. OK?

JIMMY exits. MACEY sits. Pause.

MOHAMMED: Is pretty girl… Meryl?

MACEY: Meryl, yeah.

MOHAMMED: And other girl is…?

MACEY: Cheryl.

MOHAMMED: Cheryl. And boy is…?

MACEY: Daryl.

MOHAMMED: Meryl. Cheryl. Daryl. All sound same. Why all sound same?

MACEY: It's a long story.

MOHAMMED: There is time before I get deport. (*Pause.*) There is time for story.

Pause.

MACEY: There's a place in Wales called Rhyl.

MOHAMMED: Rhyl?

MACEY: It's by the seaside. It's crap really. And tacky. And horrible. But I had the best day of me life there. (*Little pause.*) It was the last holiday I had with me dad.

MOHAMMED: Your father.

MACEY: Yeah. (*Pause.*) One great fantastic day in Rhyl… princess for a day…and then he buggered off out of me life.

MOHAMMED: Your father go away? He no come back? Why? Why would father do that?

Pause.

MACEY: Let's get on with this. What's me favourite colour?

MOHAMMED: I think you have scar people cannot see.

MACEY: Favourite colour?

MOHAMMED: Blue.

MACEY: Favourite food?

MOHAMMED: You have many scar people cannot see. (*Little pause.*) You like Chinese food.

MACEY: Favourite perfume?

MOHAMMED: Is more difficult for you when people no see scar.

MACEY: Stop it. What's me favourite perfume?

MOHAMMED: Lou Lou. Is nice perfume.

MACEY: Favourite singer?

MOHAMMED: Wombles.

MACEY: … Favourite singer?

MOHAMMED: Ms Dynamo.

MACEY: *Mite.* Ms Dyna*mite.* You have to remember all this, Mo.

MOHAMMED: I remember. No worry.

MACEY: Favourite movie.

MOHAMMED: Why cannot be Wombles?

MACEY: God Almighty, what is it with you and the Wombles?

Beat. He smiles. She smiles…then laughs.

MACEY: Have yer ever actually seen The Wombles, Mohammed?

She goes to the cardboard box, fishes out a book, gives it to MOHAMMED…

MOHAMMED: … *This* is Wombles?… But they are *rat!*… Great big rat!

MACEY: They're for kids.

MOHAMMED: … Children like rat?

MACEY: Yeah. Kids are weird.

Pause.

MOHAMMED: Hey Macey, I want show you scar.

MACEY: No.

MOHAMMED: No, is OK. Is little scar. Is good scar… Look. (*He rolls up his trouser leg.*) See? This one scar I like. It remind me of when little boy. My father, he get me bike one day. He want teach me ride bike. Put hand on shoulder. To help. I say, no father, is OK. Mohammed ride bike easy. I watch other boys ride bike. So I ride bike. Just like them. You watch. But I see look in his eye. This look say 'you are silly boy'. So I ride bike down hill. What happen?

MACEY: You fell off the bike.

MOHAMMED: Yes. I fall off bike. I bang leg on rock. Is blood all over. I scream. Scream like baby. This scar remind me of father.

MACEY: How old were you?

MOHAMMED: Twenty-two. (*Beat.*) Is joke. Age is joke. Fall off bike is for real. I about…six year I think.

Pause. MACEY lifts her skirt and shows MOHAMMED a scar on her leg.

MACEY: I got this when I was about six.

MOHAMMED: How you get?

MACEY: I fell off a wall.

MOHAMMED: Children always fall down.

MACEY: I was drunk.

MOHAMMED: Drunk? With drink?… At *six* you drunk?

MACEY: My mother liked to drink.

MOHAMMED: Your *mother* give you drink? I no understand. Why she do that?

MACEY: She had problems. (*Little pause.*) I fell off the wall and landed on a piece of broken glass.

MOHAMMED: Is very difficult to be child.

Long pause.

MACEY: Favourite movie? (*Beat.*) Favourite movie?

MOHAMMED: You like *Pretty Woman.* Is movie I no see. You think we can watch? Together?

MACEY: No. We've got work to do. I had a favourite song when I was a child. What was it?

MOHAMMED: …Was song your mother teach you.

MACEY: Yeah. But what was it called?

MOHAMMED struggles to remember. Lights down to black. Segment of 'La vie en rose' by Edith Piaf plays…

… then segues into a cacophony of foreign languages and foreign accents – men, women, children. This is the waiting room at the Court of Asylum and Immigration Appeals. A legal coat of arms is illuminated, and its motto: DIEU ET MON DROIT.

FEMALE USHER's VOICE: Mrs Ahmadi, Hearing Room Six, please. Mrs Ahmadi, Hearing Room Six.

Little pause. Silence.

MALE ADJUDICATOR's VOICE: (*Rather pompous and condescending.*) Ah… Mrs Ahmadi, there you are. It's very good of you to join us. I've heard so much about you. Won't you please take a seat?

Scene Twenty-Eight

The Bistro. Late Afternoon.

JIMMY at one table on his mobile phone. SAMIR at another table, his accordion on the floor.

JIMMY: Cliff… Cliff… I can't…really… I would but I can't…because…no, it's not that I don't…

CHERYL enters carrying a bowl of soup and a roll on a plate. She's wearing her baseball cap, peak pulled down. She walks very slowly, her head is bowed, her hands are shaking, and she's muttering to herself.

JIMMY: Cliff…just shut up a minute would you… I've got Cheryl here…yes…*here*…at the bistro…yeah…and I can't…well, I can't very well leave her alone can I?… Isn't there someone else you can call?

Suddenly, a cannon of bangers and fireworks from outside. CHERYL starts and drops the bowl of soup and the roll.

CHERYL: Oh! Oh! Oh!

JIMMY: Cliff, I've got to go. I'll check on you later.

JIMMY rushes to CHERYL.

CHERYL: Oh! Look what I did!

JIMMY: It's OK.

CHERYL: But look what I did!

JIMMY: It's not a problem.

CHERYL: I'm no good at this. What am I doing here? I'm making a mess.

JIMMY: You're doing fine.

CHERYL: No I'm not. I'm not doing fine. I'm really not. There's too much space in here. And these windows. Look at them. They're awful big. They're way too big. You didn't tell me the windows were going to be this big. I can see outside. People. Walking past. All kinds of people. And kids. Just… And cars. And trucks. And more people. I can see everything. I can hear everything.

JIMMY: Just take a seat…come on…sit down.

CHERYL: Not by the window!

JIMMY: All right. Here. Here. Take it easy. It's going to be OK.

CHERYL: There's a lot of air in here. Don't you think? So much air.

JIMMY: It's all right. You need air.

CHERYL: But I can't catch it though. I can't catch it.

JIMMY: Cheryl, remember your happy place? Yes? Remember we talked about your happy place?

CHERYL: I don't have a feckin' happy place! (Silly stupid psycho-babble!)

JIMMY: OK. OK. Deep breaths. Deep breaths now.

CHERYL: … I don't know why I let yer talk me into this.

JIMMY: Take it easy, Cheryl. OK? Everything's going to be fine. I promise you… I'll get you a glass of water.

CHERYL: Tea. I want tea.

JIMMY: OK. Tea. Right. Just try and…relax.

JIMMY exits. CHERYL begins opening sachets of sugar, emptying them on to the table. SAMIR watches her. He picks up his accordion and begins playing a soothing melody. She turns and looks at him, briefly. It seems to calm her down. JIMMY enters with a mug of tea, places it on the table. CHERYL takes the mug, holds it to the side of the table – and underneath – and brushes the sugar off the table and into the mug. JIMMY goes and picks up the broken crockery…

JIMMY: (*To SAMIR.*) I'll get you another bowl of soup.

JIMMY exits. The music is peaceful, soothing. Until…MACEY storms into the bistro, looking for JIMMY.

MACEY: Where is he?!… JIMMY!!

SAMIR stops playing.

MACEY: *JIMMY!!!!* Get yer arse out here!

JIMMY enters. MACEY's in his face.

MACEY: Where is he? Eh?

JIMMY: What's the matter?

MACEY: Where the fuck is he?

JIMMY: Who?

MACEY: Don't give me 'who'?

JIMMY: Mohammed?

MACEY: I'll wring his frigging neck. And I'll wring yours right after it.

JIMMY: Why? What is it?

MACEY: Fucking-psycho-fucking-Kurdish-fucking-loon!

JIMMY: What's *happened?!*

MACEY: If yer know where he is yer'd better tell me right now.

JIMMY: I don't know where he is. I don't.

MACEY: I'll cut his frigging nuts off when I get my hands on him.

JIMMY: Macey, will you just –

MACEY: Don't touch me!

Little pause.

JIMMY: Will you just *tell* me what he's done.

MACEY: He's run off with me kids!

JIMMY: … What?! Mohammed?… No. That's im-… Run off where?

MACEY: If I knew that I wouldn't be here talking to you, would I? Yer stupid bloody man.

SAMIR comes over…

MACEY: I'm warning yer Jimmy. I'm holding yer personally responsible. If anything happens to me kids. I mean it. If I find so much as one single hair out of place I'll hunt yer down like a scabby dog.

SAMIR: Excuse. I hear what you say. There is no need for worry.

MACEY: Who *the fuck* are you?

SAMIR: I am friend of Mohammed.

MACEY: Do yer know where he is?… No? Then keep yer nose out.

JIMMY: Macey, take it easy. Mohammed wouldn't harm your kids. He just wouldn't.

SAMIR: Jimmy is right.

MACEY: YER DON'T KNOW THAT! Yer don't know what state of mind he's in. He could be capable of anything.

She tries to light up a cigarette. She has difficulty because her hands are shaking. JIMMY lights it for her.

JIMMY: The two of you went to the Courts?… Right?… Right?

MACEY: Yeah! We went to the Courts!

JIMMY: … *And?*

MACEY: And it was bloody horrible. (*Little pause.*) Standing there, getting the third degree, like we were some…like *I* was…just by *looking* at us yer could tell what they thought…bunch of toffee-nosed-stuck-up-their-own-arses-chinless-fucking-wonders!… They treated us like we were something they'd just walked in. And I've never heard such shite in all me life… (*Exaggerated posh accent:*)… 'Irarq… Kurdistarn…terribly difficult of course, but, well, things improving all the time, don't you know. Dawn of a whole new era.' Blah blah blah. Fuckers. And his *solicitor*…some geeky little Harry Potter look-a-like…he didn't know his arse from a hole in the ground.

JIMMY: … They didn't go for it?…They didn't go for the story?

MACEY: Well, they *might* have done had soft ollies been able to learn his lines. He was all over the show. Dates. Times. Places. Couldn't remember anything. (Poor bastard.)

Stammering… shaking… the amount of sweat on his face, yer could have grown rice!

SAMIR: They send Mohammed back? Is what you are saying? They deport Mohammed?

Little pause. MACEY takes a letter from her purse.

MACEY: Mohammed can stay… I got them to change their minds.

Little pause.

SAMIR: How you do this?

MACEY: Never you fucking mind 'how I do this!' (*To JIMMY:*) So. I'm in there. Right. With Lord-fucking-Haw-Haw. I'm getting his bloody letter for him. And I come out. And he's gone. Straight to the school.

SAMIR: … Maybe Mohammed take children home.

MACEY: Yer think I didn't *go* home?!

JIMMY: Macey…there must be some explanation.

MACEY: Nobody goes near my kids but *me,* Jimmy. No one. Well, I'm telling yer, he can stick his frigging letter!

MACEY rips the letter to shreds, throws them on the floor.

CHERYL: (*Head down.*) Oh. Oh. Oh.

MACEY: What's her problem?

CHERYL: Oh God oh God oh God.

JIMMY: She's…overwrought. Look. Just sit down a minute. Let's think this through. Sit. I'll get you a drink.

MACEY: Brandy. Make it a big one.

JIMMY exits. Pause.

What's got *you* so overwrought?

CHERYL rises and exits to the kitchen.

SAMIR: Really Macey. There is no need for worry. Mohammed, he is good man. Believe. He has good heart.

JIMMY enters with a glass of brandy. MACEY knocks it back in one go.

SAMIR: Mohammed, he love children.

Sound of violin from kitchen. It's beautiful. They all turn to look. MOHAMMED enters, stands on their blind side...

MOHAMMED: Is pretty tune.

MACEY turns back and sees MOHAMMED, leaps out of her chair and grabs hold of him.

MACEY: What have yer done with me kids?! Where are they?!

MOHAMMED: Ow! What you do?!

MACEY: Where are me kids?

MOHAMMED: They are *home!*

MACEY: No they're not! I've been home.

MOHAMMED: I just take. *Now.* Believe. Kids are safe!...What is problem, Macey?

MACEY: Stay away from me kids. D'yer hear me? Don't *ever* go near me kids.

Pause.

MOHAMMED: Woman at Court, she say you and judge, you might be long time in office. Talking. I see clock on wall. I remember you need get kids from school. So...I do this for you, Macey. So they no have to wait. So you no worry. I get kids and I take home. But they want to go to park. They make big noise for go to park. They pull Mohammed...so...we go and feed duck. (*Little pause.*) I call you on phone. I leave message for you.

She takes a mobile phone from her pocket and looks at it.

MOHAMMED: You no get message?

MACEY: ... I brought the wrong phone.

MOHAMMED: Please?

MACEY: I brought the wrong phone.

Pause.

MOHAMMED: You still no trust? Is what you feel?

MACEY: I don't know yer.

Pause.

MOHAMMED: I sorry, Macey. Big sorry. I know is last time I see kids. Before I go. I will have good memory.

MACEY: Yer not going.

MOHAMMED: Man from Immigration, the judge, he no care.

MACEY: He signed yer letter.

MOHAMMED: … What you say?

MACEY: The judge signed yer letter… Yer can stay.

MOHAMMED: Is true?

MACEY: Indefinite leave.

MOHAMMED: Mohammed can remain in country?

MACEY: Yer can stay for good.

MOHAMMED: Where is letter?

MACEY points to the floor…

JIMMY: I'll get some sellotape.

JIMMY exits. MOHAMMED falls to his knees.

MOHAMMED: *This* is letter allow me to stay?

MACEY kneels down. They pick up the pieces together.

You make judge change his mind?… He listen to you?

MACEY: Yeah. He listened.

MOHAMMED begins to cry.

MOHAMMED: I no think this happen. (*Pause.*) You are good friend, Macey. (*Pause.*) You are good friend.

Scene Twenty-Nine

Hospital Ward. Evening.

Two beds. CLIFF in one bed, battered and bruised, holding a bunch of flowers. An overnight bag on the bed. In the other bed, a patient with his head and face completely covered in bandages. Sitting at CLIFF's bedside, MARVIN. He looks uneasy.

CLIFF: What's the matter with you?

MARVIN: I can't stand hospitals. They make me queasy.

CLIFF: You don't have to stay on my account.

> *Pause.*

MARVIN: It's not very attractive you know.

CLIFF: What?

MARVIN: Sulking.

CLIFF: I'm not sulking.

MARVIN: You *look* like you're sulking.

> *Pause.*

CLIFF: The flowers are lovely. Thank you.

> *Pause.*

MARVIN: When you get out of here I'm going to give you some boxing lessons.

CLIFF: Boxing. Me?

MARVIN: Yeah. Then maybe you won't be such an easy target for muggers.

> *Long pause.*

CLIFF: I wasn't mugged. (*Pause.*) I lied. (*Pause.*) I got myself into a situation.

MARVIN: What sort of situation?

CLIFF: I was drunk. And off me tits on something I shouldn't have taken.

MARVIN: Where was this?

CLIFF: Club.

MARVIN: Which club?

CLIFF: You don't want to know.

Pause.

MARVIN: So, you were out on the town. Sulking. And skulking. In dark corners? Very mature.

Pause.

CLIFF: I didn't *do* anything. (*Pause.*) I'm like this because I wouldn't do anything.

MARVIN: So why did you go?

CLIFF: I don't know. Because…

MARVIN: Because…?

CLIFF: Because I needed to feel…wanted. Wanted to feel… needed.

CLIFF mimes retching at his own mawkishness. Pause.

MARVIN: Why has everything always got to be about you? What *you* want? What *you* need?

CLIFF: Because I'm scared! All right?… I'm bloody petrified. (*Pause.*) That's what living alone does to you.

Pause. MARVIN takes CLIFF's hand…

(*Withdrawing his hand.*) Careful. No Public Displays of Affection. We don't want your image tarnished.

MARVIN takes CLIFF's hand again. Pause.

What's got into you?

The man in the other bed lets out a moan.

MARVIN: What happened to him?

CLIFF: Not sure. Think some yobs threw fireworks in his face.

MARVIN: Christ. This city. (*Pause. Looks at his watch.*) I've got to go.

CLIFF: So soon?

MARVIN: I've got a date.

CLIFF: … Oh?

MARVIN: With my mum.

CLIFF: Oh… Anywhere nice?

MARVIN: Don't laugh… We're going to the opera.

CLIFF laughs, but it's painful.

MARVIN: It was *her* idea.

CLIFF: Which opera?

MARVIN: I don't know. Something Italian.

Little pause.

CLIFF: You'll come tomorrow?

MARVIN: I'll come tomorrow… Oh. (*Takes an envelope from his pocket.*) Here.

CLIFF: …What's this?

MARVIN: Things I like about you.

MARVIN exits. CLIFF opens the envelope, takes out a sheaf of papers: this is way more than 'ten things'. Pause. STELLA enters with a Styrofoam cup of coffee. She has a black eye and a few bruises, and has been crying. She sits by the other bed. She takes hold of BEHROUZ's hand…

CLIFF: Is he going to be all right? Your boyfriend.

STELLA: … I don't know.

Scene Thirty

Street. MACEY's Flat. Early evening.

Darkness. Sound of Cathedral bells. Fade. Lights up on MACEY and

MOHAMMED sat on the bench, coats on, drinking tea. Sound of children playing, off. Contented pause.

MOHAMMED: Is big fuck-off church, yes?

MACEY: … What?

MOHAMMED: (*Pointing.*) Church. Is very very big.

MACEY: It's called a cathedral.

MOHAMMED: Cathedral. What is difference?

MACEY: … I don't know. It's bigger. God's got more room to stretch his legs.

MOHAMMED: And church at other end of street?

MACEY: That's a cathedral too.

MOHAMMED: Liverpool have *two* cathedral?

MACEY: Yeah. We're schizophrenic.

MOHAMMED: Please?

MACEY: Forget it.

Pause.

MOHAMMED: Liverpool very rich to have *two* big fuck-off cathedral.

MACEY laughs.

What?

MACEY: Nothing.

MOHAMMED: Something.

MACEY: Yer make me laugh.

MOHAMMED: Is good, no?

MACEY: Is good, yes.

Pause. A ball comes bouncing on from the wings. MOHAMMED picks it up and throws it back.

MOHAMMED: Hey kids! Five more minute! Then homework! Cheryl! You no pull face, will stick like that.

He sits on bench again. Pause. He practically beams with contentment.

Is nice here. Is peaceful.

A police siren speeds past. This doesn't seem to disturb MOHAMMED's sense of well-being.

Sky is pretty tonight.

SANDRA – a neighbour of MACEY's – walks past… leading a goat on a rope.

SANDRA: Macey.

MACEY: Sandra.

SANDRA exits with the goat. MOHAMMED is wide-eyed. He rises from the bench, looks off.

MOHAMMED: Is goat!

MACEY: Yeah.

MOHAMMED: Is real goat!

MACEY: Mad isn't it?

MOHAMMED: Why she have goat?

MACEY: One of her kids wanted one so… She's off her head that one.

MOHAMMED: Off her cak-k-ke! Big time. (*Little pause.*) One year in Liverpool, is first goat I see.

MOHAMMED sits. Pause. MOHAMMED shivers conspicuously, moves a little closer to MACEY. Pause.

Macey…

MACEY: No.

Pause.

MOHAMMED: No?

MACEY: No.

Pause.

MOHAMMED: Is definite, no?

Long pause.

MACEY: Yer can sleep on the couch.

Pause. MOHAMMED smiles.

MOHAMMED: OK. I sleep on couch. Is beginning. (*Pause.*) Is beginning.

MOHAMMED starts whistling the Womble song.

Lights slowly fade to black.

The End.

A Note on the Staging

This play was written and structured as a three act play with very deliberate act breaks. However, the play can be performed with a single interval. I would suggest the following revised scene order to accommodate this (removing Mohammed from Scene 18):

Pre-show: Outside the theatre.

Act One

Scene 1: Split scene: Cheryl's bed sit / Cliff's bed sit / Dover.
Scene 2: Jimmy's flat – kitchen.
Scene 3: Samir's flat – living room.
Scene 4: Tower block roof.
Scene 5: Cheryl's bed sit.
Scene 6: Jimmy's bistro.
Scene 7: Macey's flat – kitchen.
Scene 8: Split scene: Cheryl's bed sit / Cliff's bed sit.
Scene 9: Great Homer Street market.
Scene 10: Sam's Office.
Scene 11: Split scene: Jimmy's bistro / kitchen.
Scene 12: Garden at Cliff's house.
Scene 13: Street outside Macey's flat.
Scene 14: Kitchen at Cliff and Cheryl's house
Scene 15: Back room of a pub.
Scene 16: Kitchen at Cliff and Cheryl's house.
Scene 17: Macey's flat – kitchen.

Act Two

Scene 18: A street.
Scene 19: Hotel Imperial. Laundry Room.
Scene 20: Cliff's bed sit.
Scene 21: Jimmy's bistro.
Scene 22: Kitchen at Cliff and Cheryl's house.
Scene 23: Registry Office.
Scene 24: Split scene: Sefton Park / Cemetery.
Scene 25: Jimmy's bistro.
Scene 26: Cheryl's bed sit.
Scene 27: Macey's flat – kitchen.
Scene 28: Jimmy's bistro.
Scene 29: Hospital room.
Scene 30: Street outside Macey's flat.